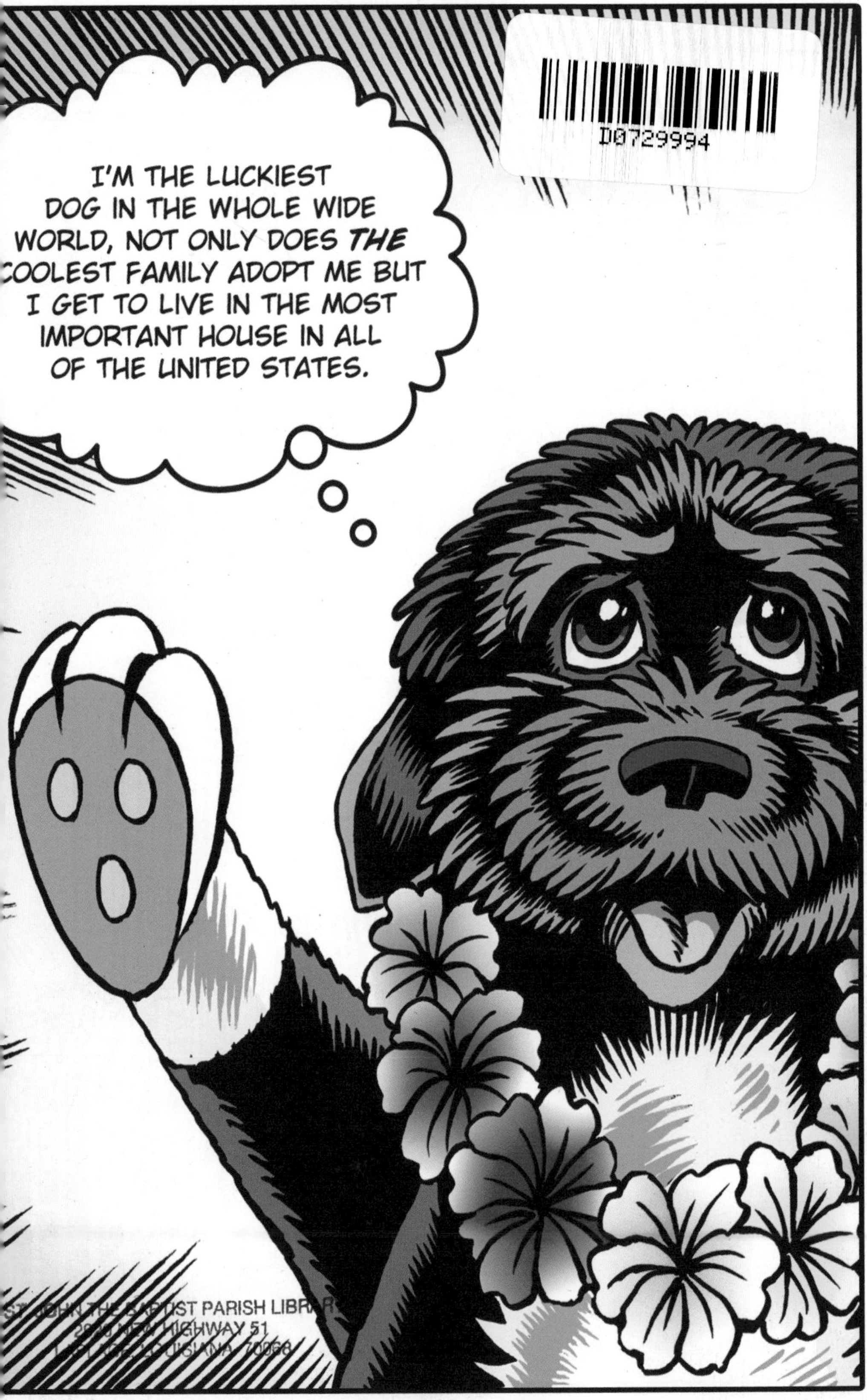
I'M THE LUCKIEST DOG IN THE WHOLE WIDE WORLD, NOT ONLY DOES *THE* COOLEST FAMILY ADOPT ME BUT I GET TO LIVE IN THE MOST IMPORTANT HOUSE IN ALL OF THE UNITED STATES.

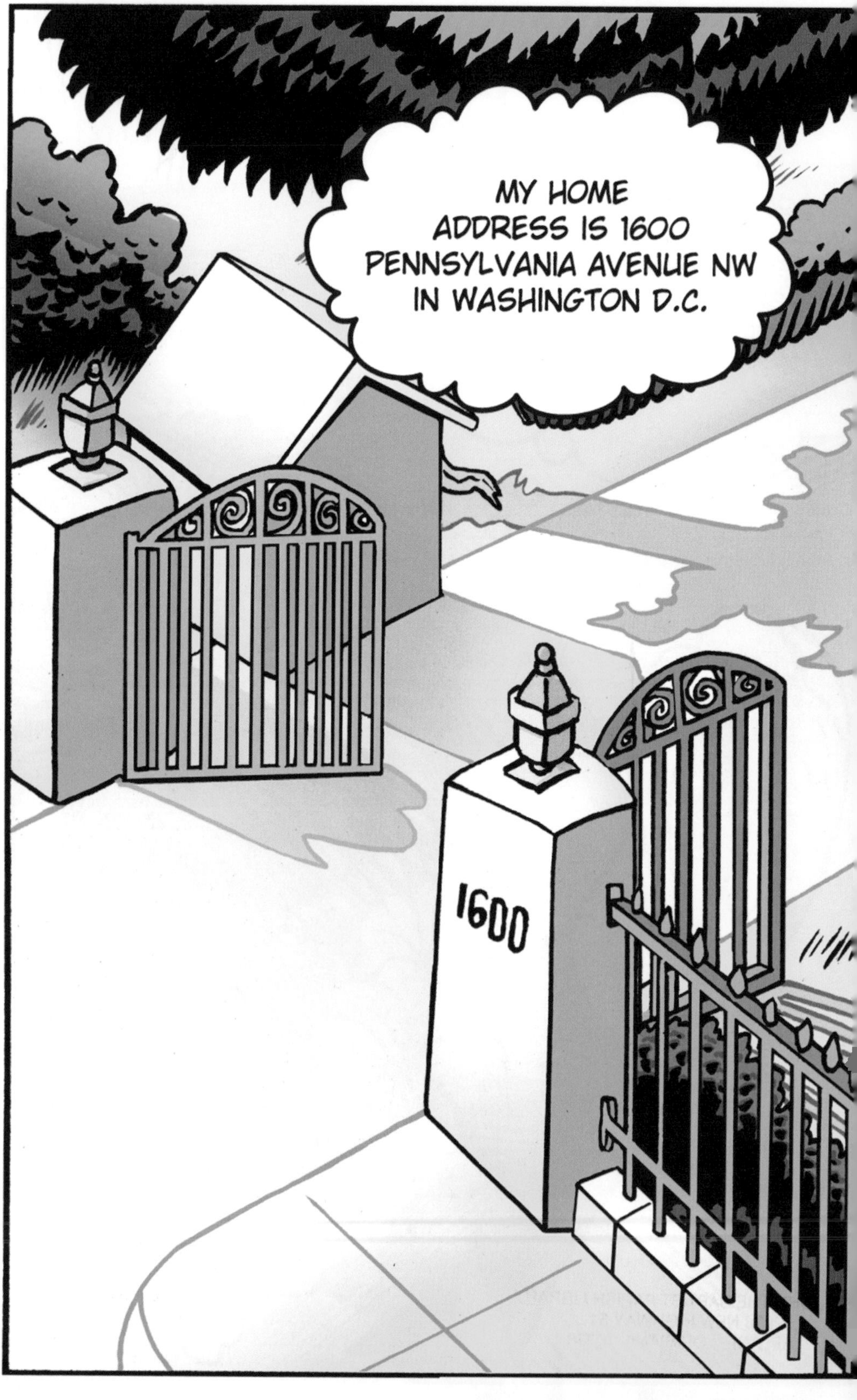
MY HOME ADDRESS IS 1600 PENNSYLVANIA AVENUE NW IN WASHINGTON D.C.
1600

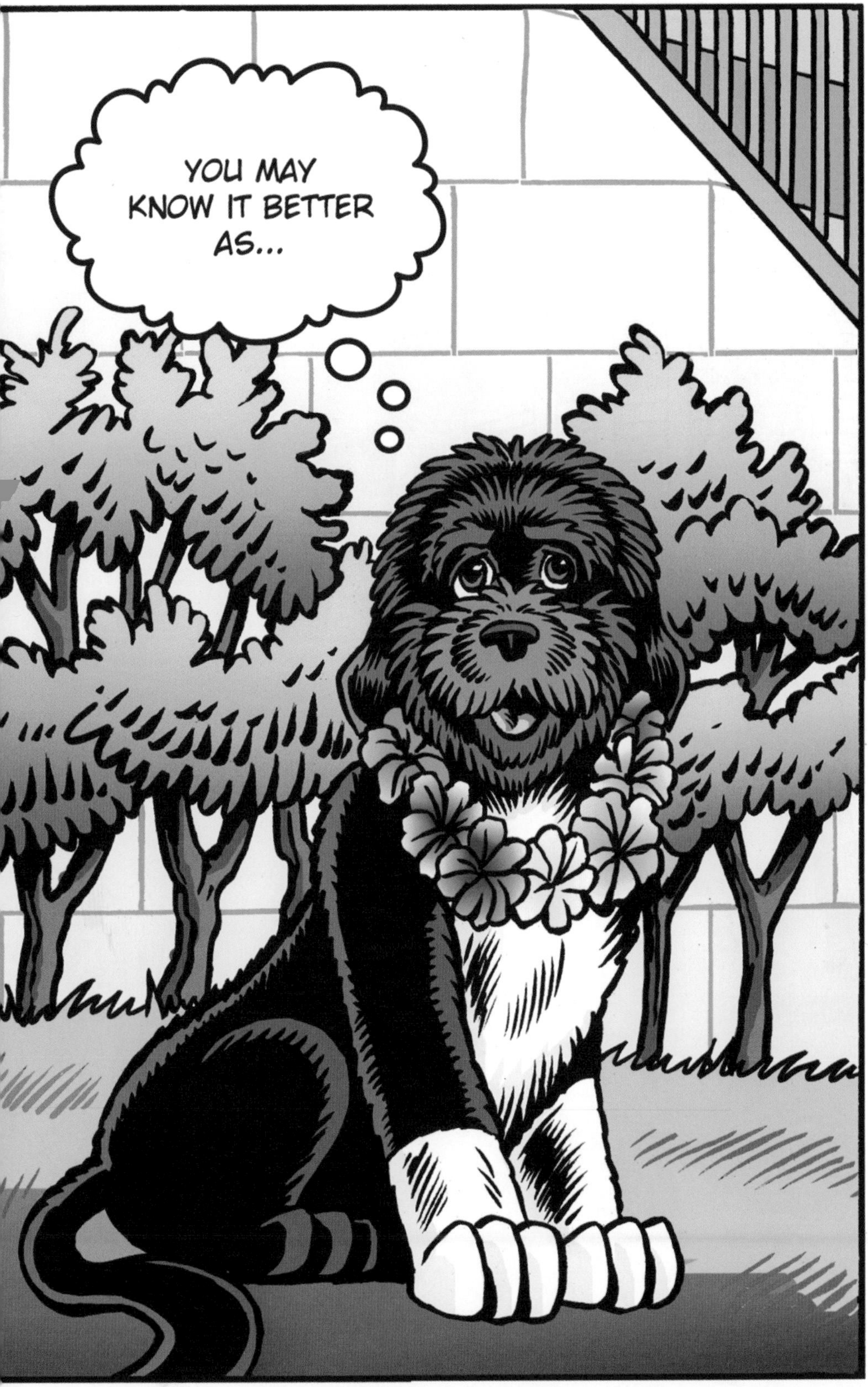
YOU MAY KNOW IT BETTER AS...

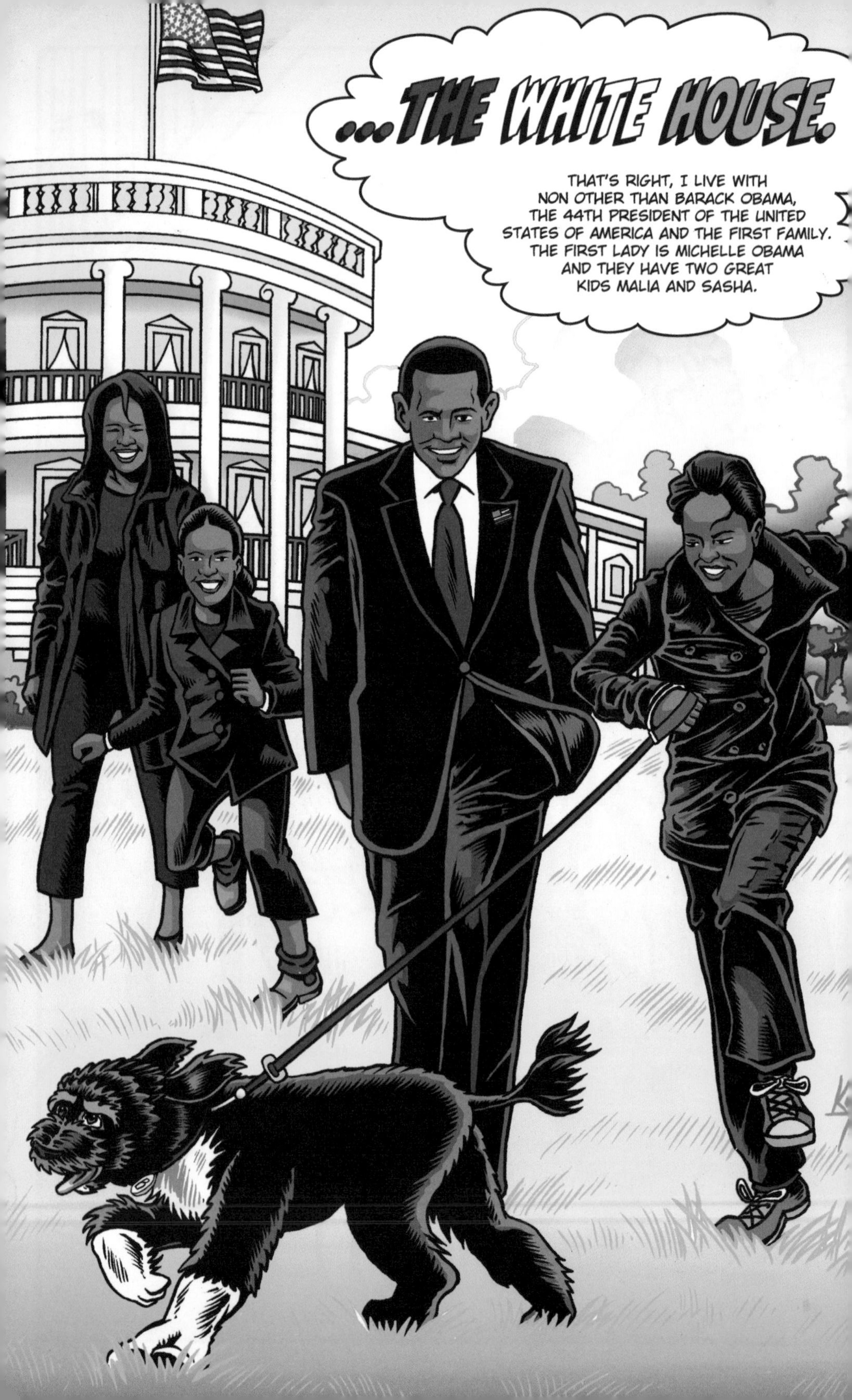
...THE WHITE HOUSE.
THAT'S RIGHT, I LIVE WITH NON OTHER THAN BARACK OBAMA, THE 44TH PRESIDENT OF THE UNITED STATES OF AMERICA AND THE FIRST FAMILY. THE FIRST LADY IS MICHELLE OBAMA AND THEY HAVE TWO GREAT KIDS MALIA AND SASHA.

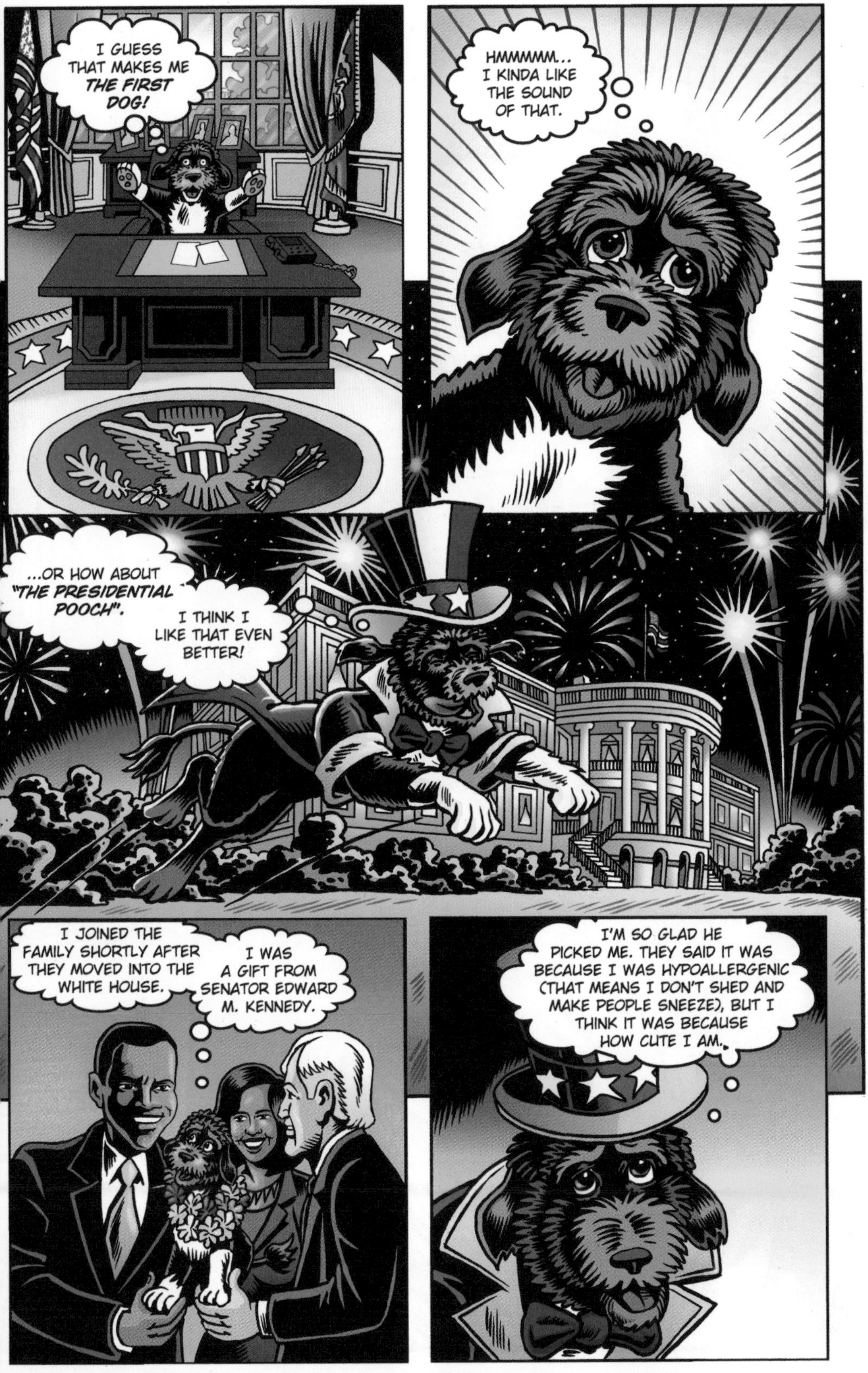
I GUESS THAT MAKES ME *THE FIRST DOG!*
HMMMMM... I KINDA LIKE THE SOUND OF THAT.
...OR HOW ABOUT *"THE PRESIDENTIAL POOCH"*.
I THINK I LIKE THAT EVEN BETTER!
I JOINED THE FAMILY SHORTLY AFTER THEY MOVED INTO THE WHITE HOUSE.
I WAS A GIFT FROM SENATOR EDWARD M. KENNEDY.
I'M SO GLAD HE PICKED ME. THEY SAID IT WAS BECAUSE I WAS HYPOALLERGENIC (THAT MEANS I DON'T SHED AND MAKE PEOPLE SNEEZE), BUT I THINK IT WAS BECAUSE HOW CUTE I AM.

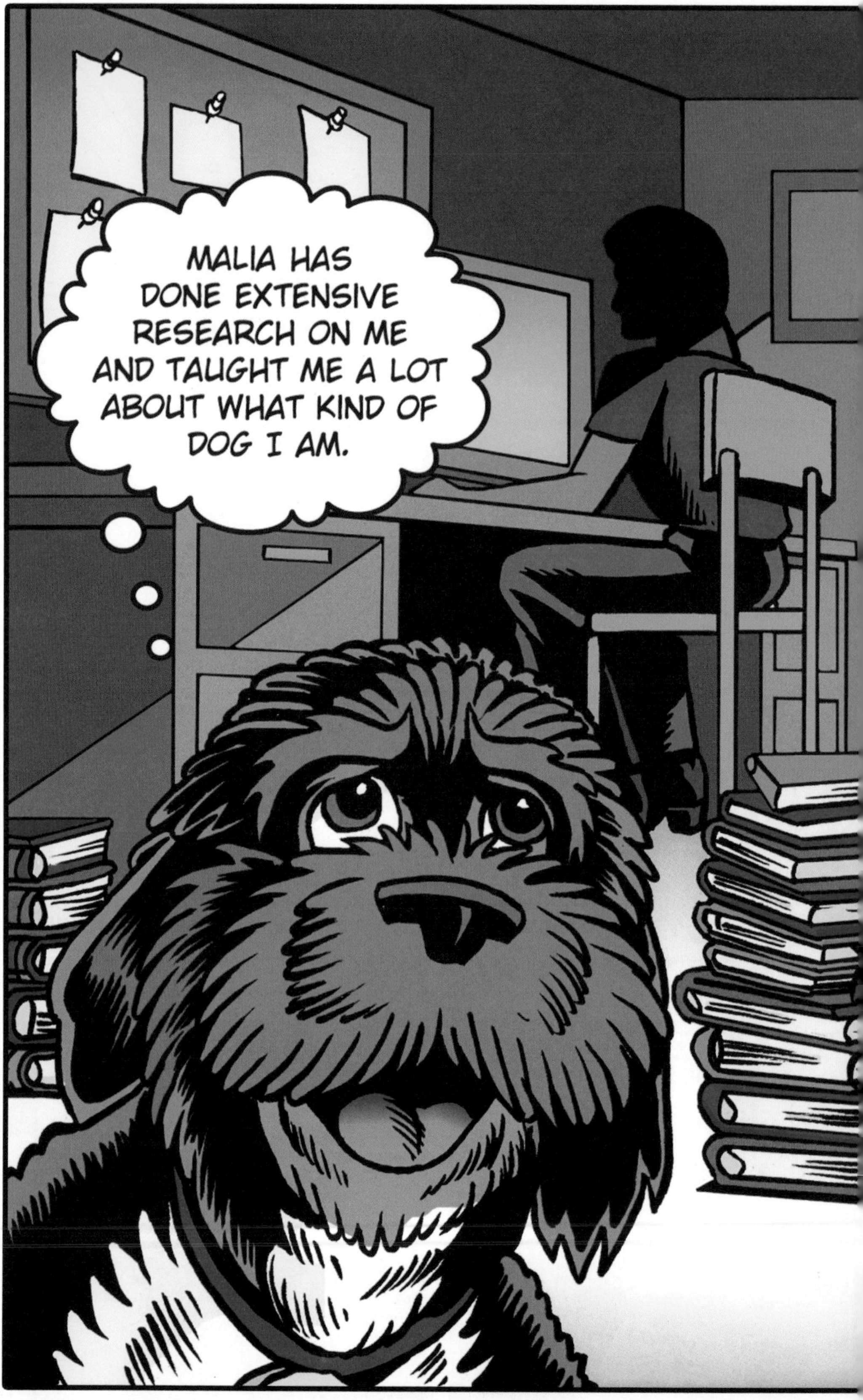
MALIA HAS DONE EXTENSIVE RESEARCH ON ME AND TAUGHT ME A LOT ABOUT WHAT KIND OF DOG I AM.

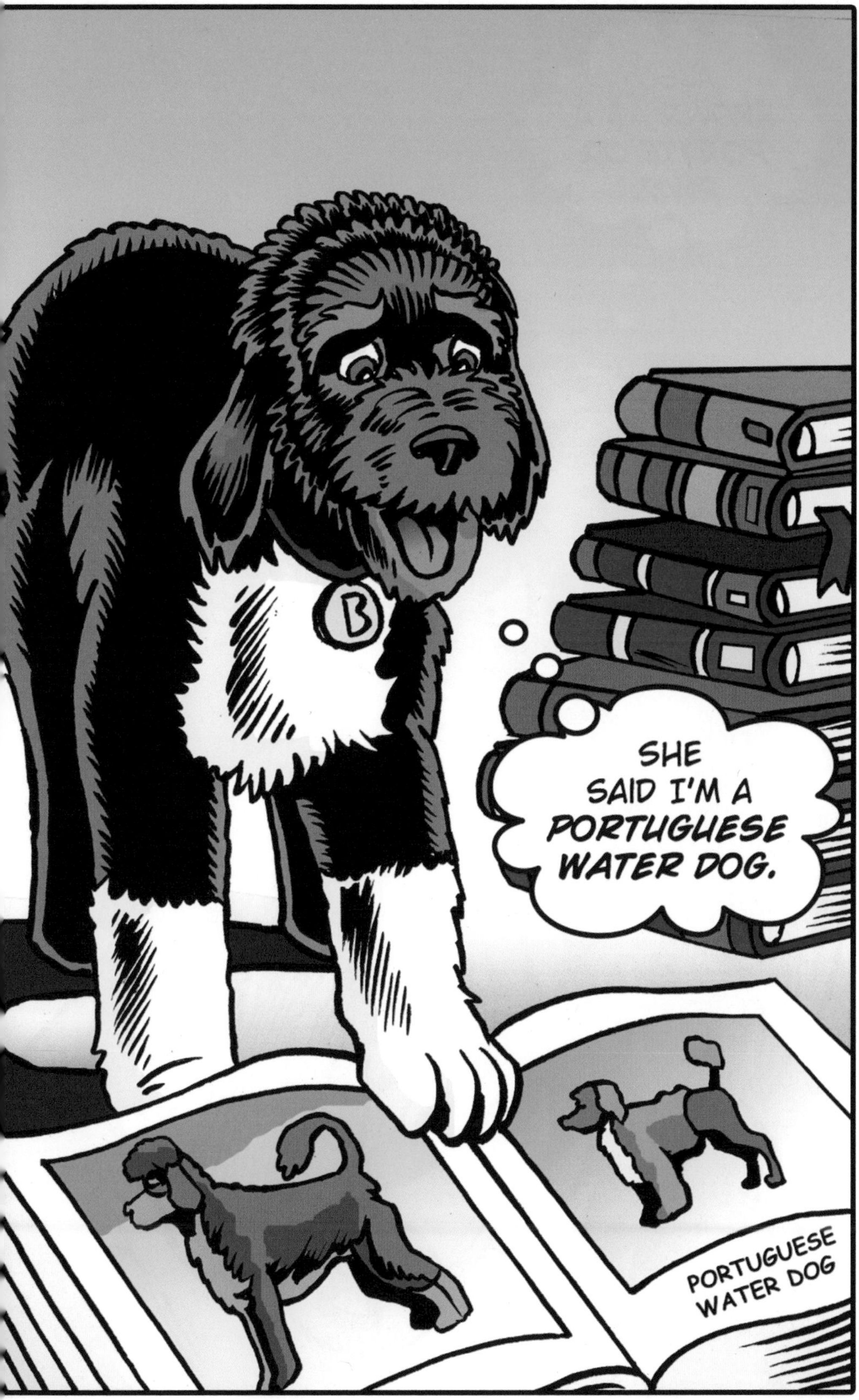
SHE SAID I'M A PORTUGUESE WATER DOG.
PORTUGUESE WATER DOG

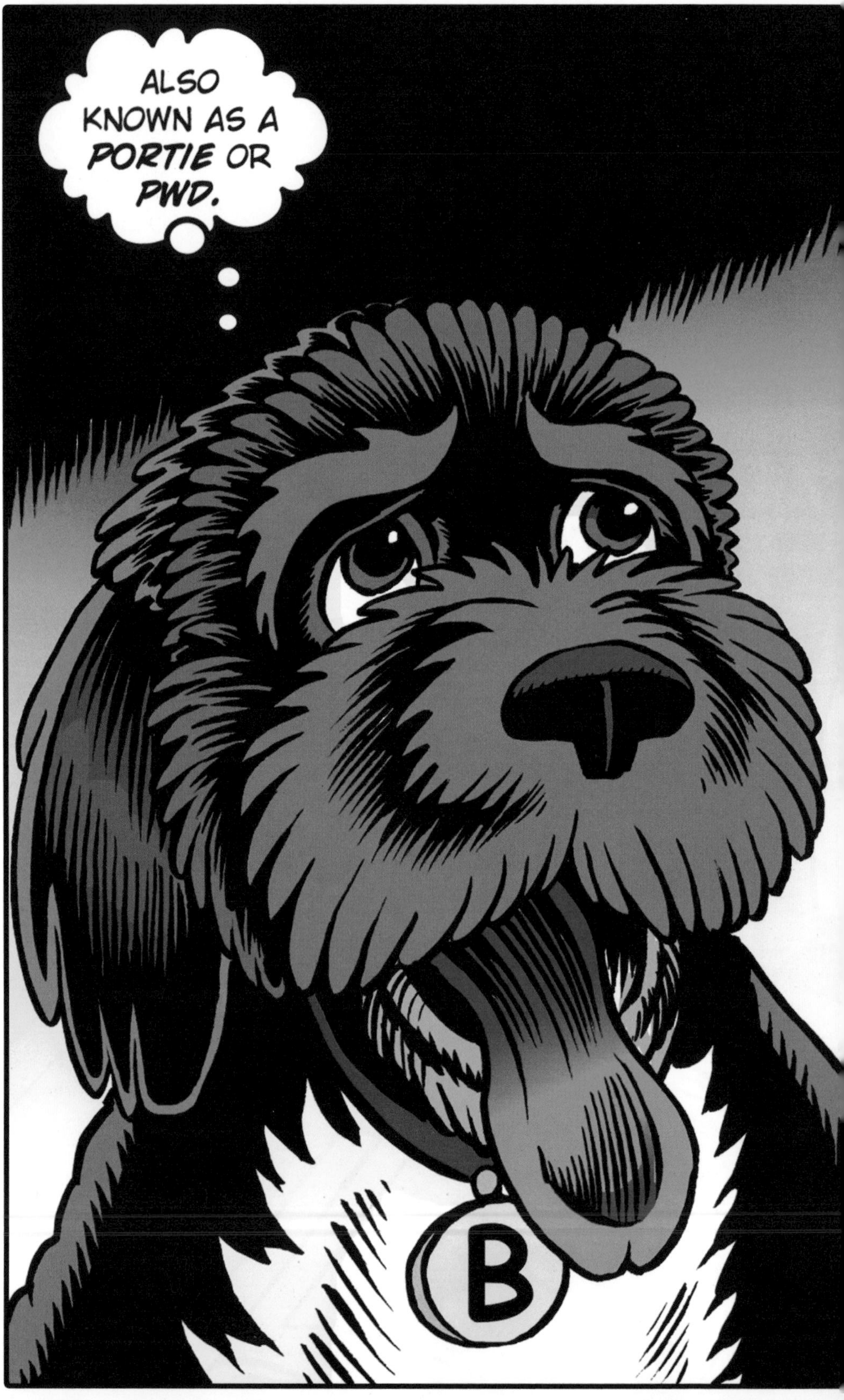
ALSO KNOWN AS A PORTIE OR PWD.

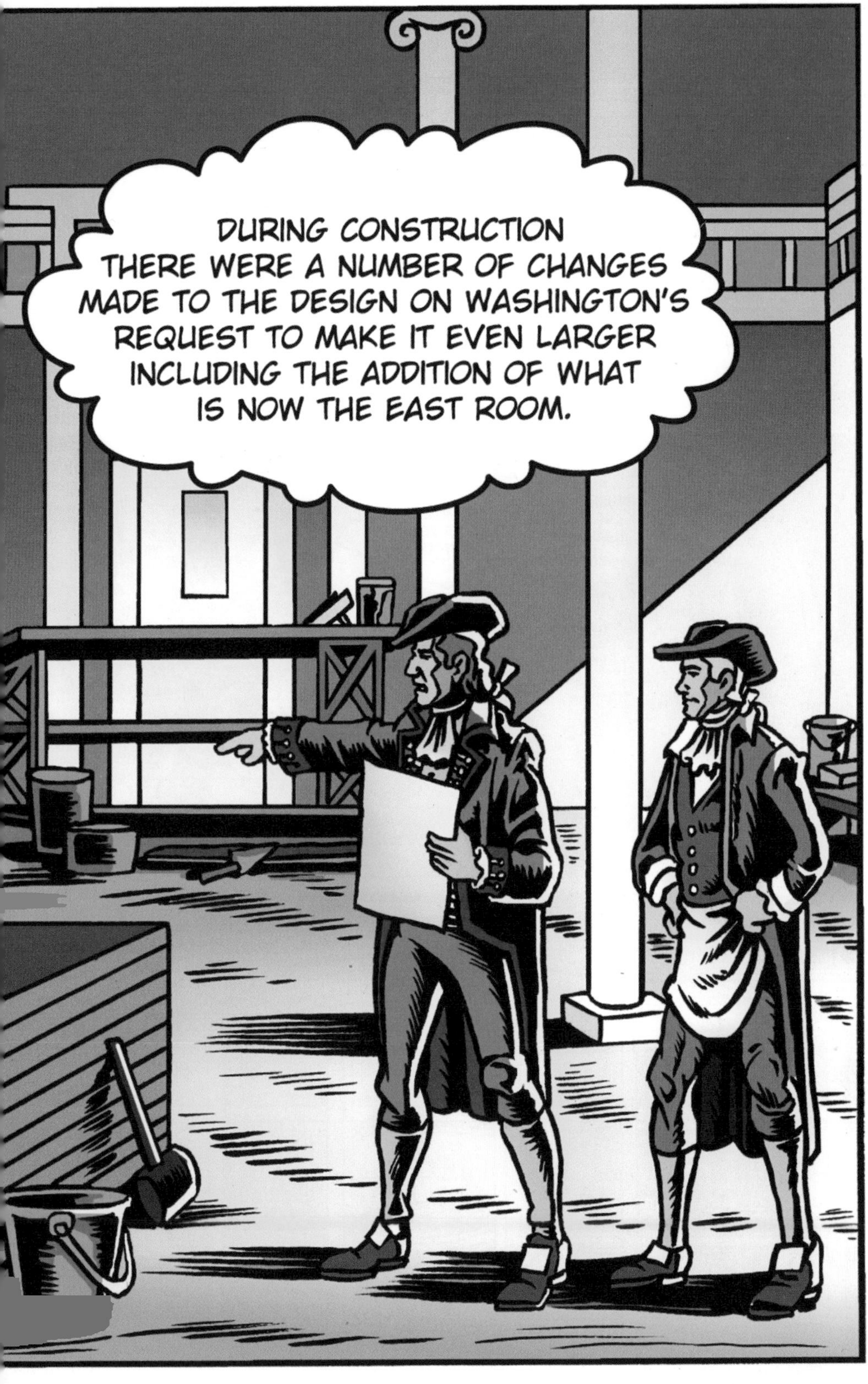
DURING CONSTRUCTION THERE WERE A NUMBER OF CHANGES MADE TO THE DESIGN ON WASHINGTON'S REQUEST TO MAKE IT EVEN LARGER INCLUDING THE ADDITION OF WHAT IS NOW THE EAST ROOM.

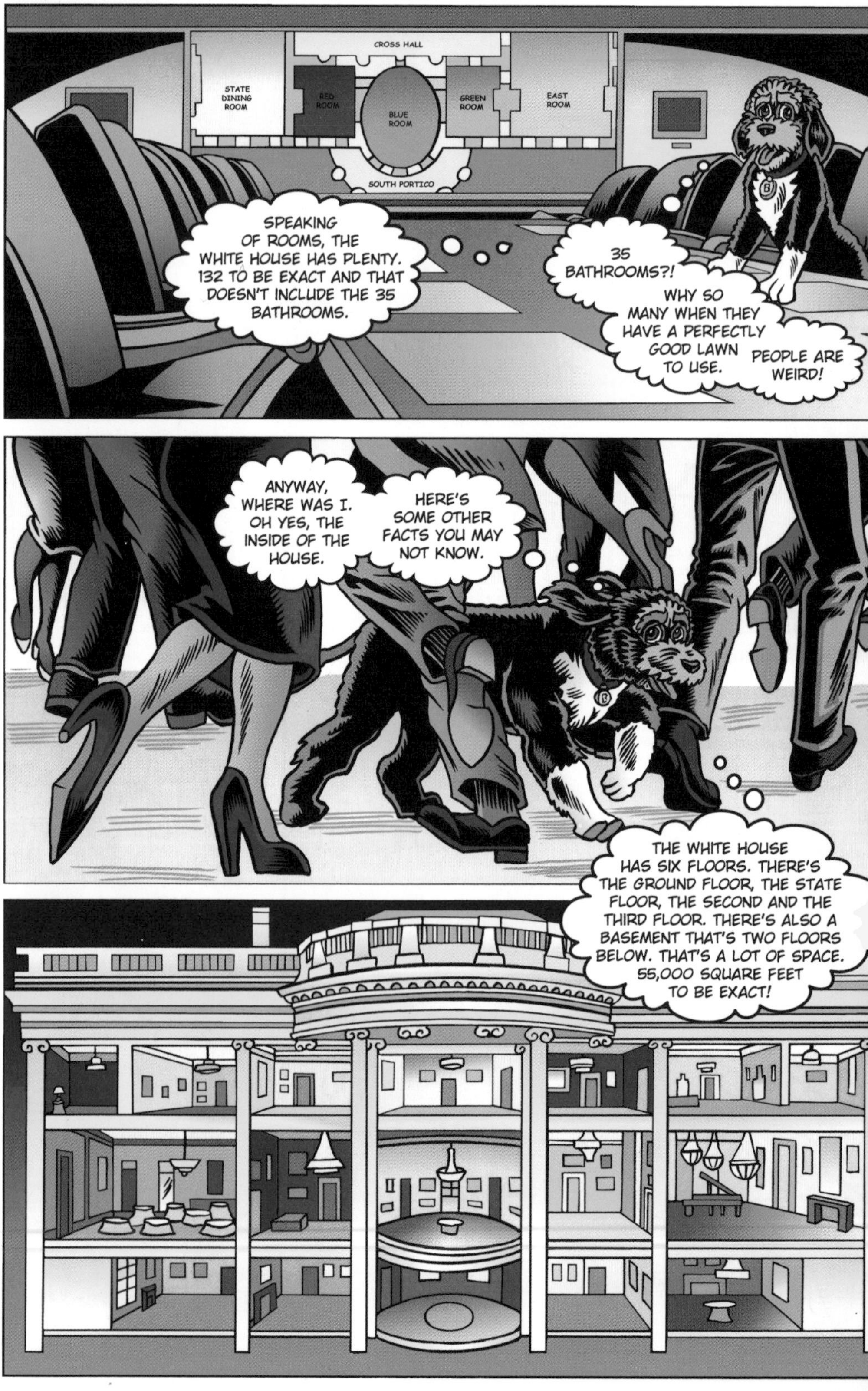
CROSS HALL
STATE DINING ROOM
RED ROOM
BLUE ROOM
GREEN ROOM
EAST ROOM
SOUTH PORTICO
SPEAKING OF ROOMS, THE WHITE HOUSE HAS PLENTY. 132 TO BE EXACT AND THAT DOESN'T INCLUDE THE 35 BATHROOMS.
35 BATHROOMS?!
WHY SO MANY WHEN THEY HAVE A PERFECTLY GOOD LAWN TO USE.
PEOPLE ARE WEIRD!
ANYWAY, WHERE WAS I. OH YES, THE INSIDE OF THE HOUSE.
HERE'S SOME OTHER FACTS YOU MAY NOT KNOW.
THE WHITE HOUSE HAS SIX FLOORS. THERE'S THE GROUND FLOOR, THE STATE FLOOR, THE SECOND AND THE THIRD FLOOR. THERE'S ALSO A BASEMENT THAT'S TWO FLOORS BELOW. THAT'S A LOT OF SPACE. 55,000 SQUARE FEET TO BE EXACT!

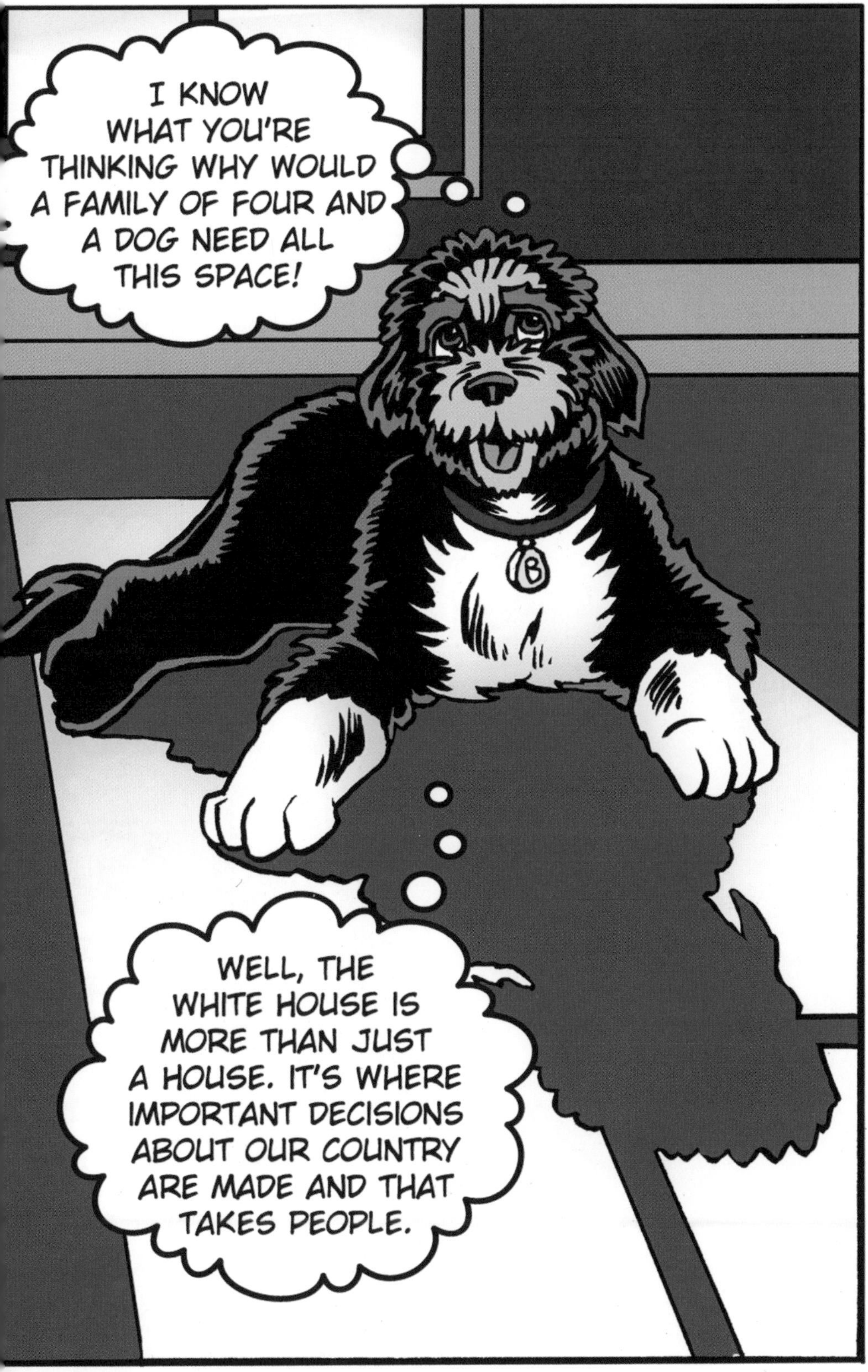
I KNOW WHAT YOU'RE THINKING WHY WOULD A FAMILY OF FOUR AND A DOG NEED ALL THIS SPACE!
WELL, THE WHITE HOUSE IS MORE THAN JUST A HOUSE. IT'S WHERE IMPORTANT DECISIONS ABOUT OUR COUNTRY ARE MADE AND THAT TAKES PEOPLE.

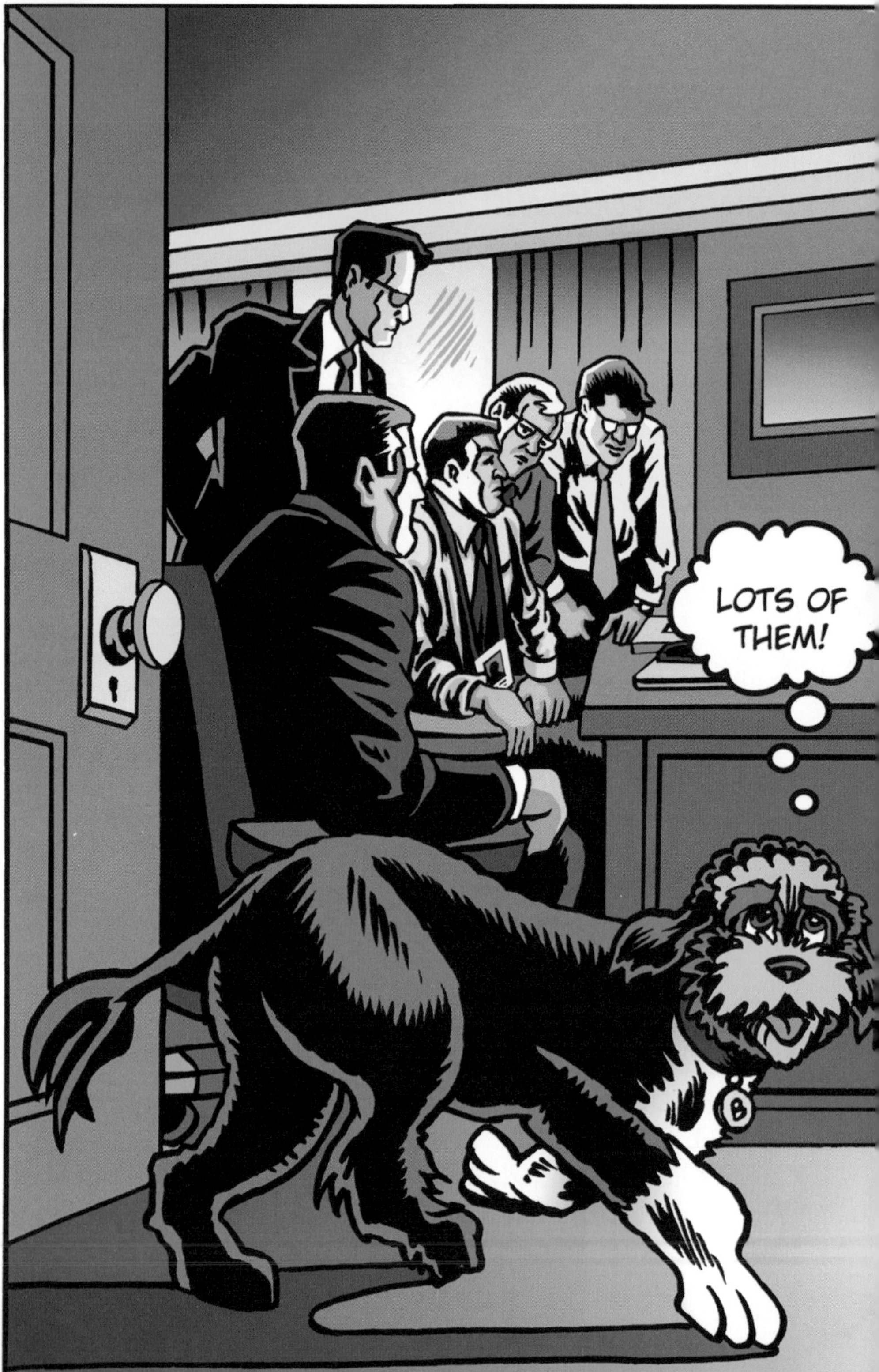
LOTS OF THEM!

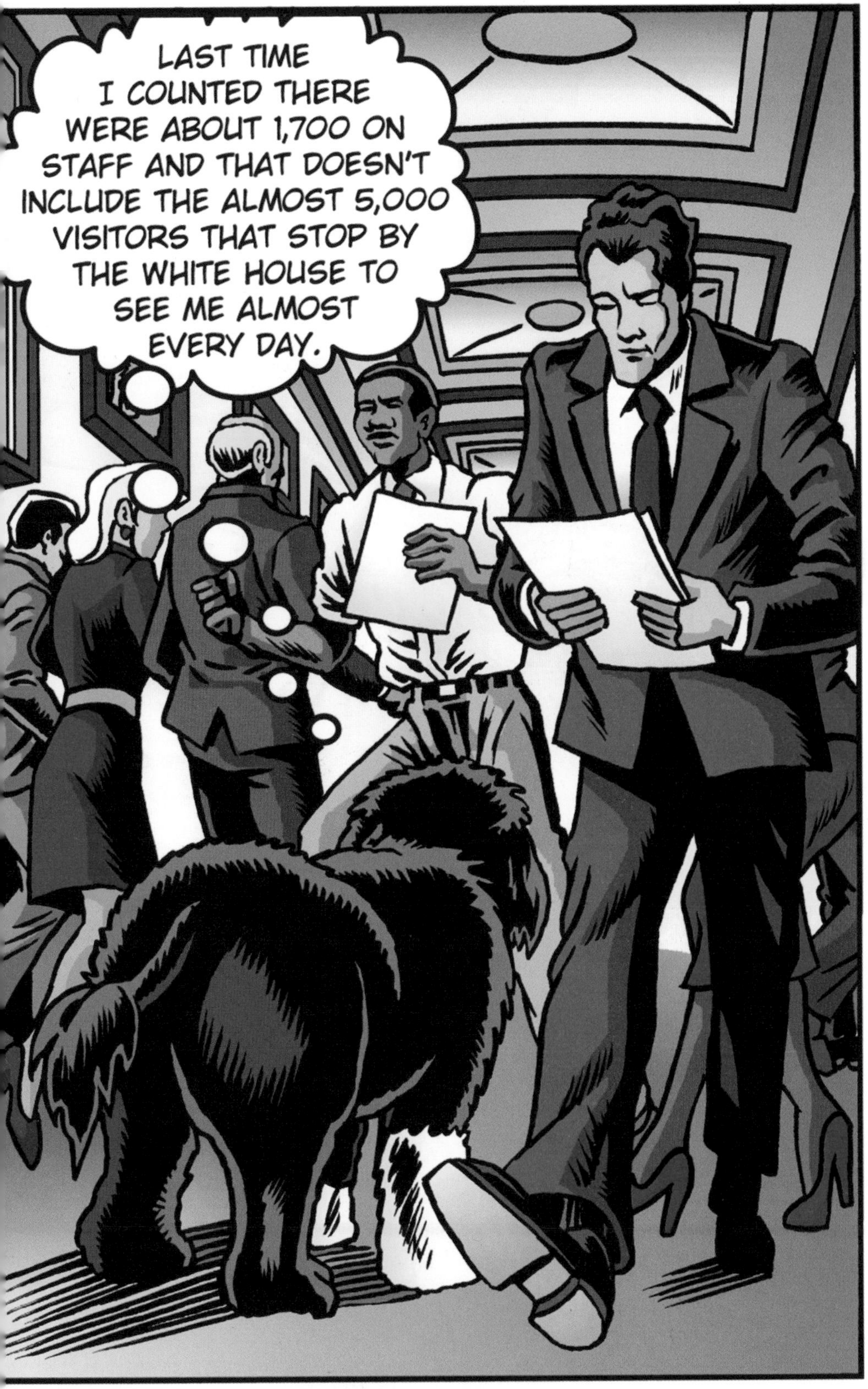
LAST TIME I COUNTED THERE WERE ABOUT 1,700 ON STAFF AND THAT DOESN'T INCLUDE THE ALMOST 5,000 VISITORS THAT STOP BY THE WHITE HOUSE TO SEE ME ALMOST EVERY DAY.

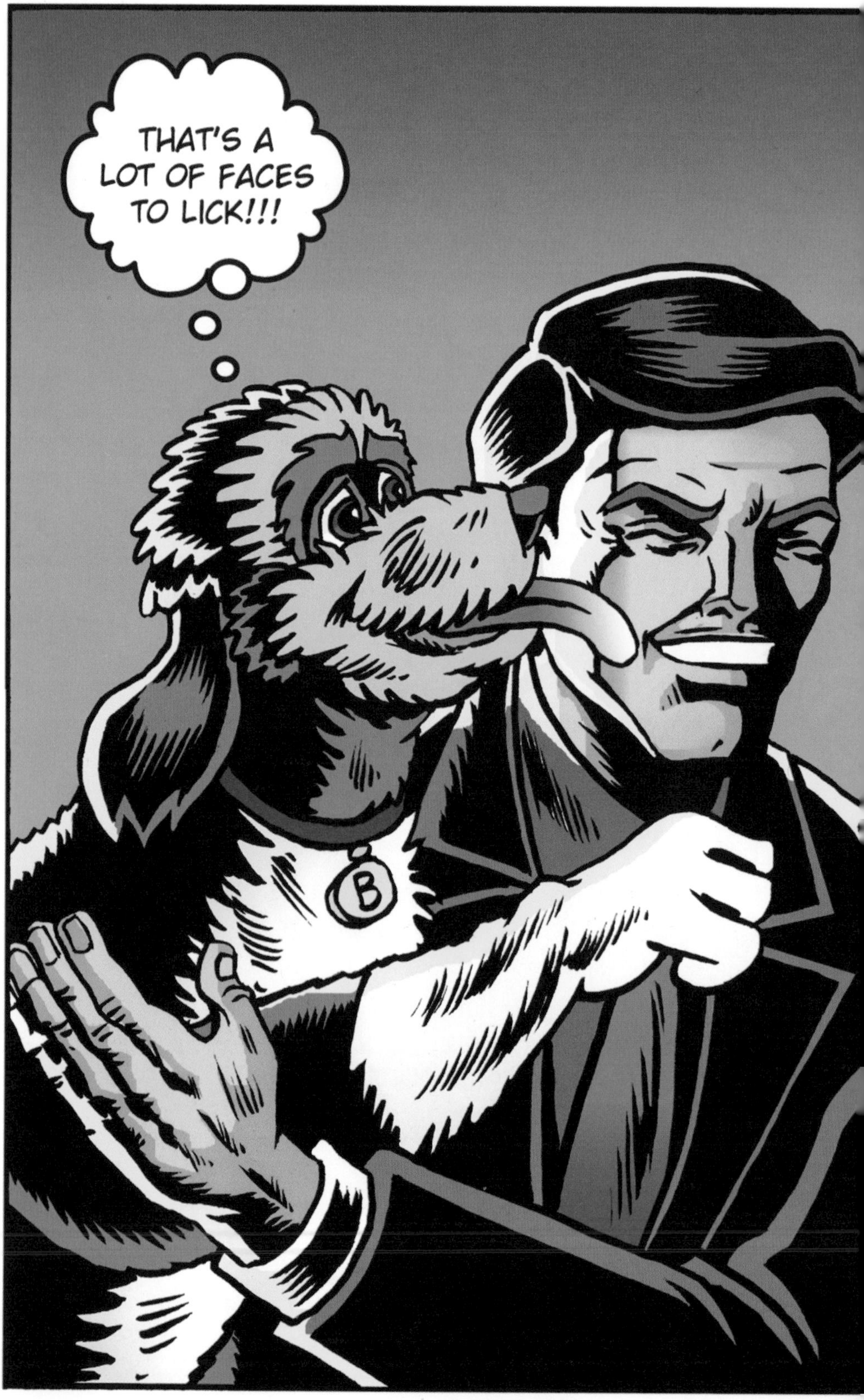
THAT'S A LOT OF FACES TO LICK!!!

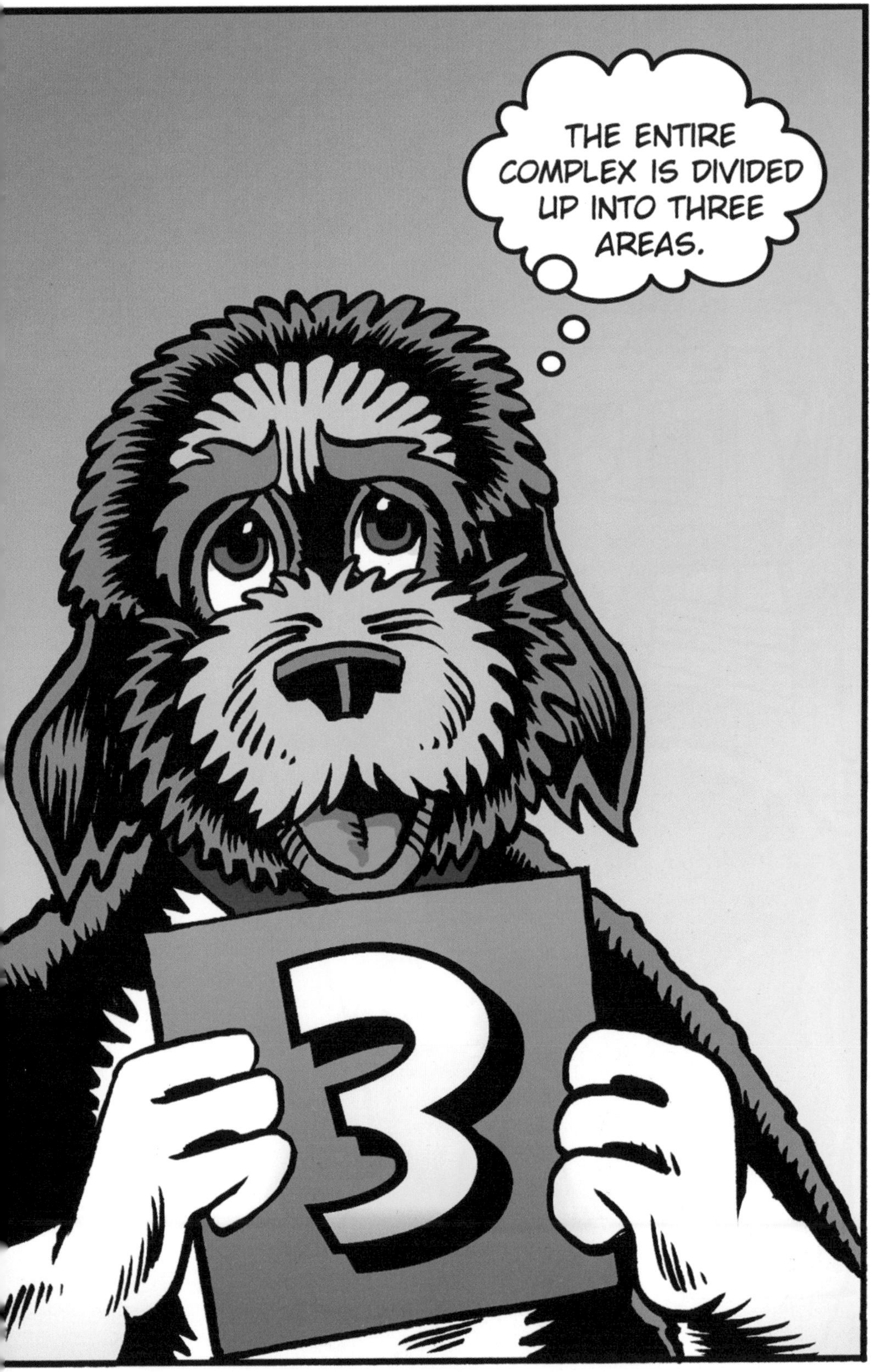
THE ENTIRE COMPLEX IS DIVIDED UP INTO THREE AREAS.
3

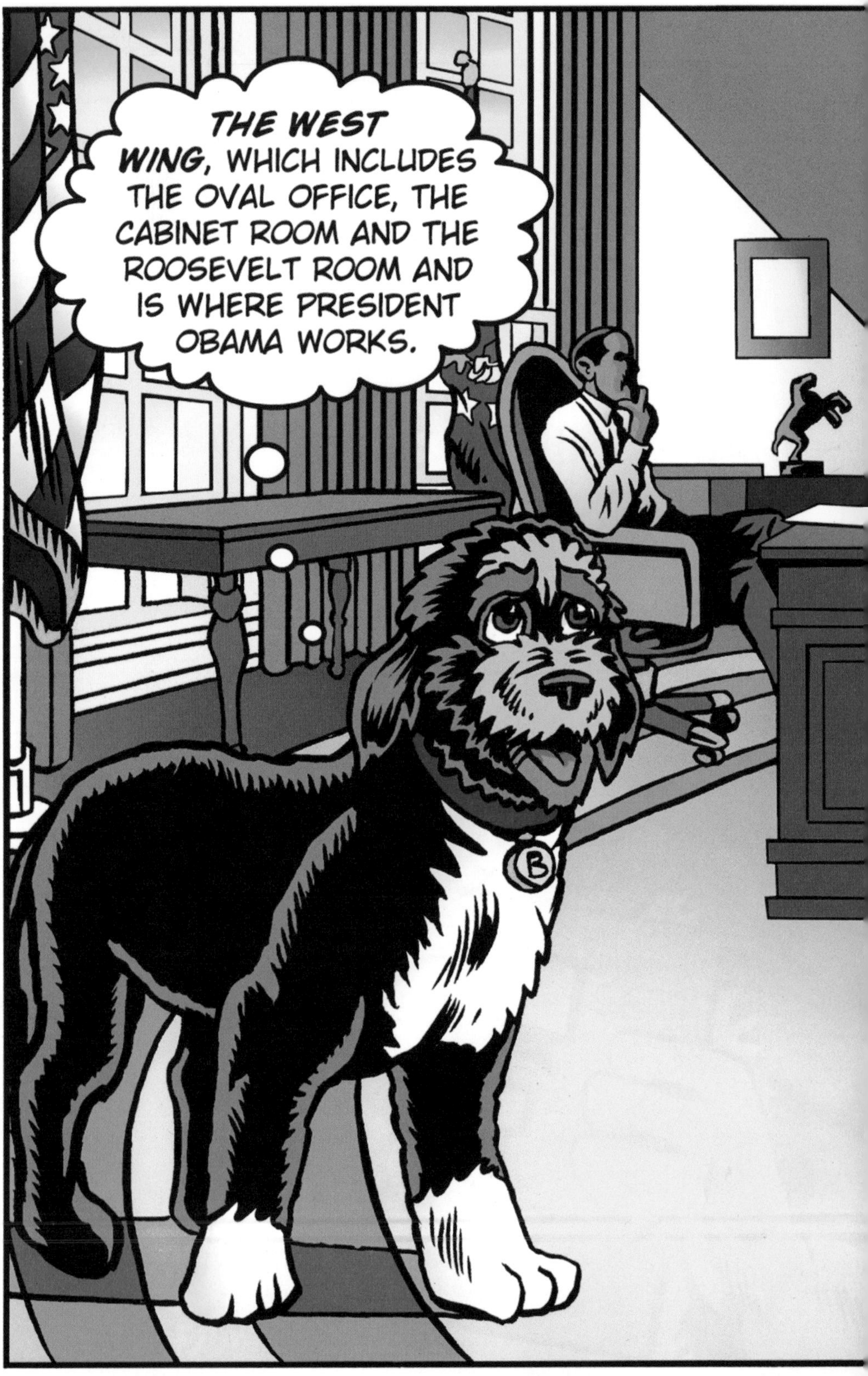
THE WEST WING, WHICH INCLUDES THE OVAL OFFICE, THE CABINET ROOM AND THE ROOSEVELT ROOM AND IS WHERE PRESIDENT OBAMA WORKS.

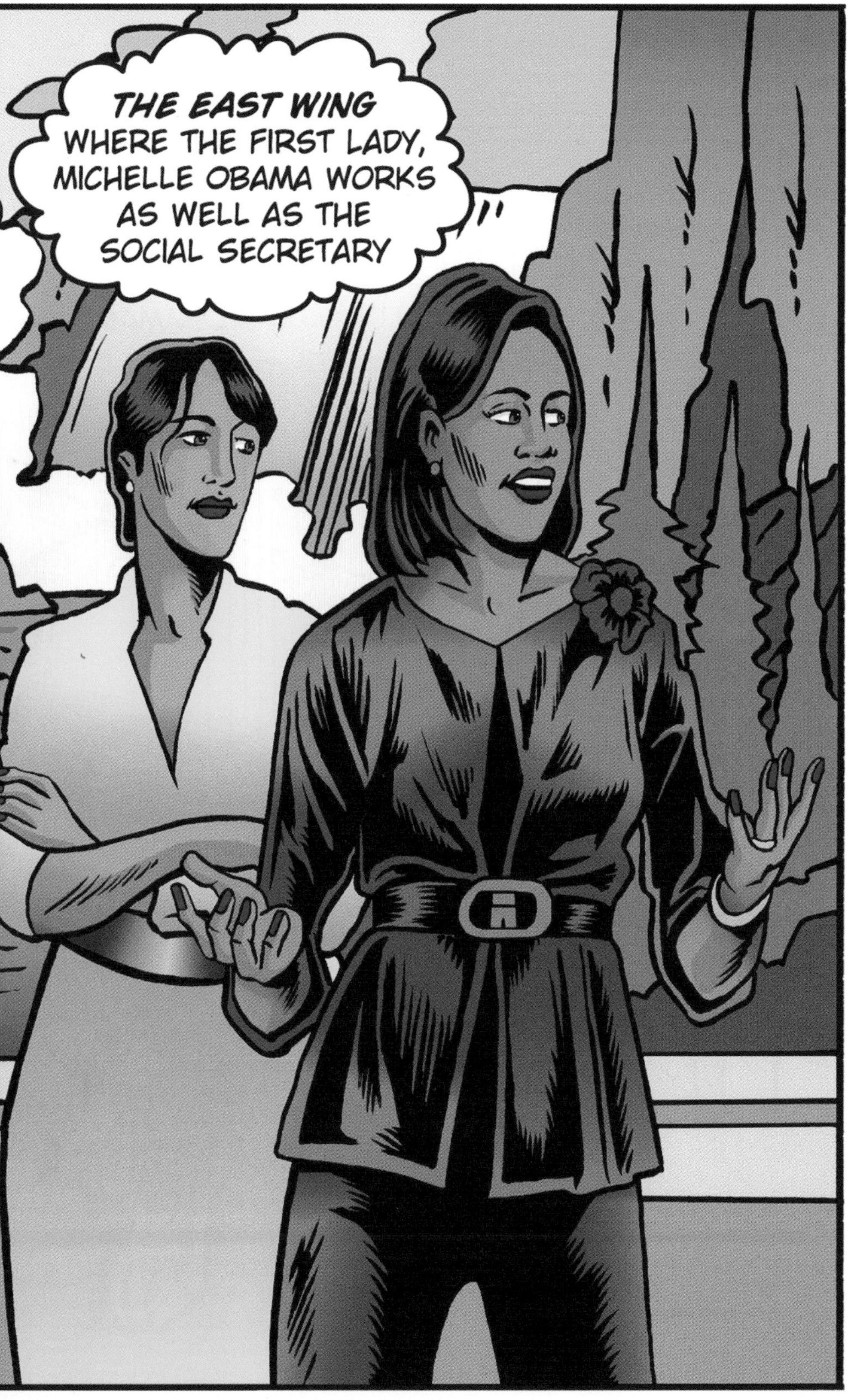
THE EAST WING WHERE THE FIRST LADY, MICHELLE OBAMA WORKS AS WELL AS THE SOCIAL SECRETARY

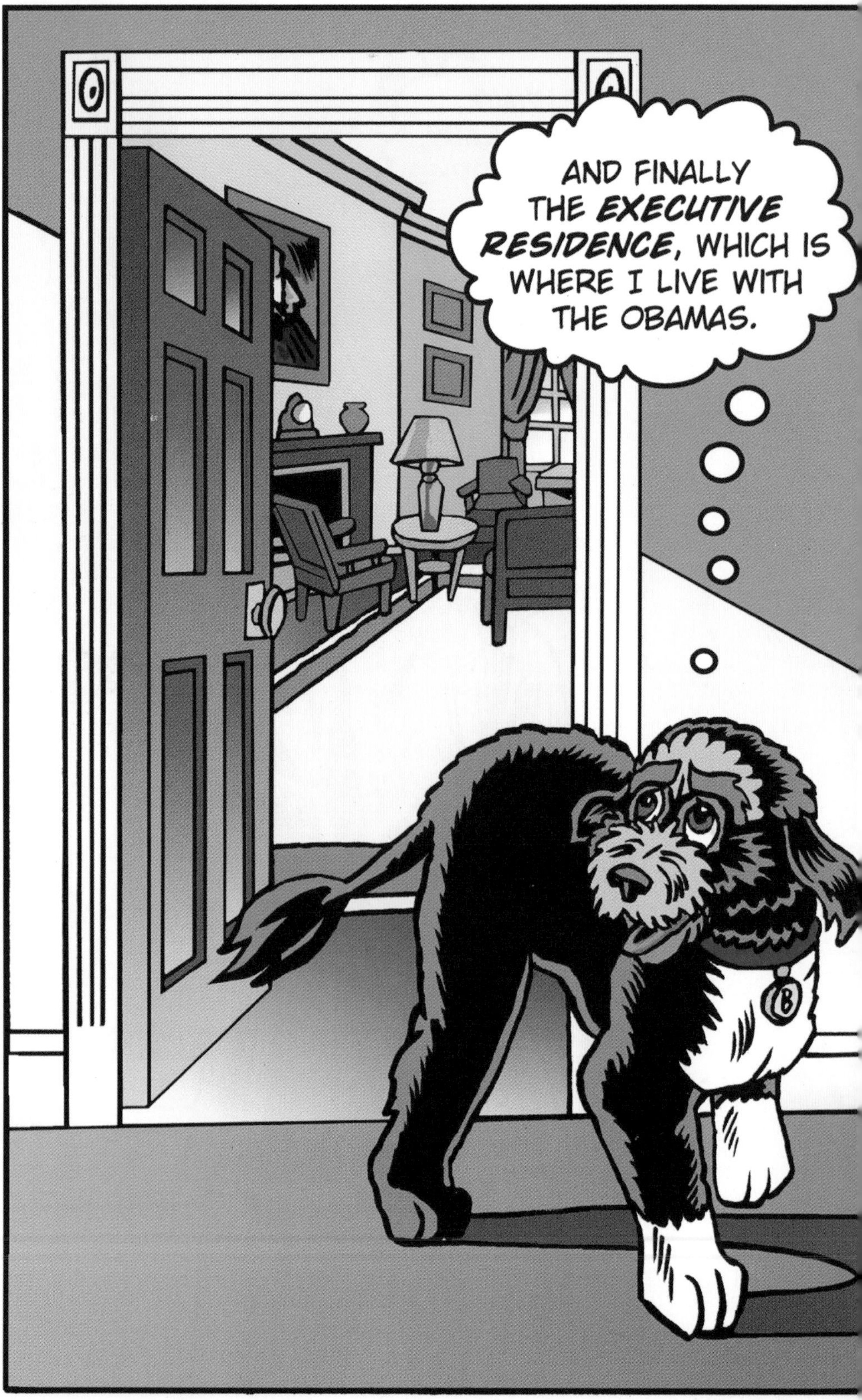
AND FINALLY THE ***EXECUTIVE RESIDENCE***, WHICH IS WHERE I LIVE WITH THE OBAMAS.

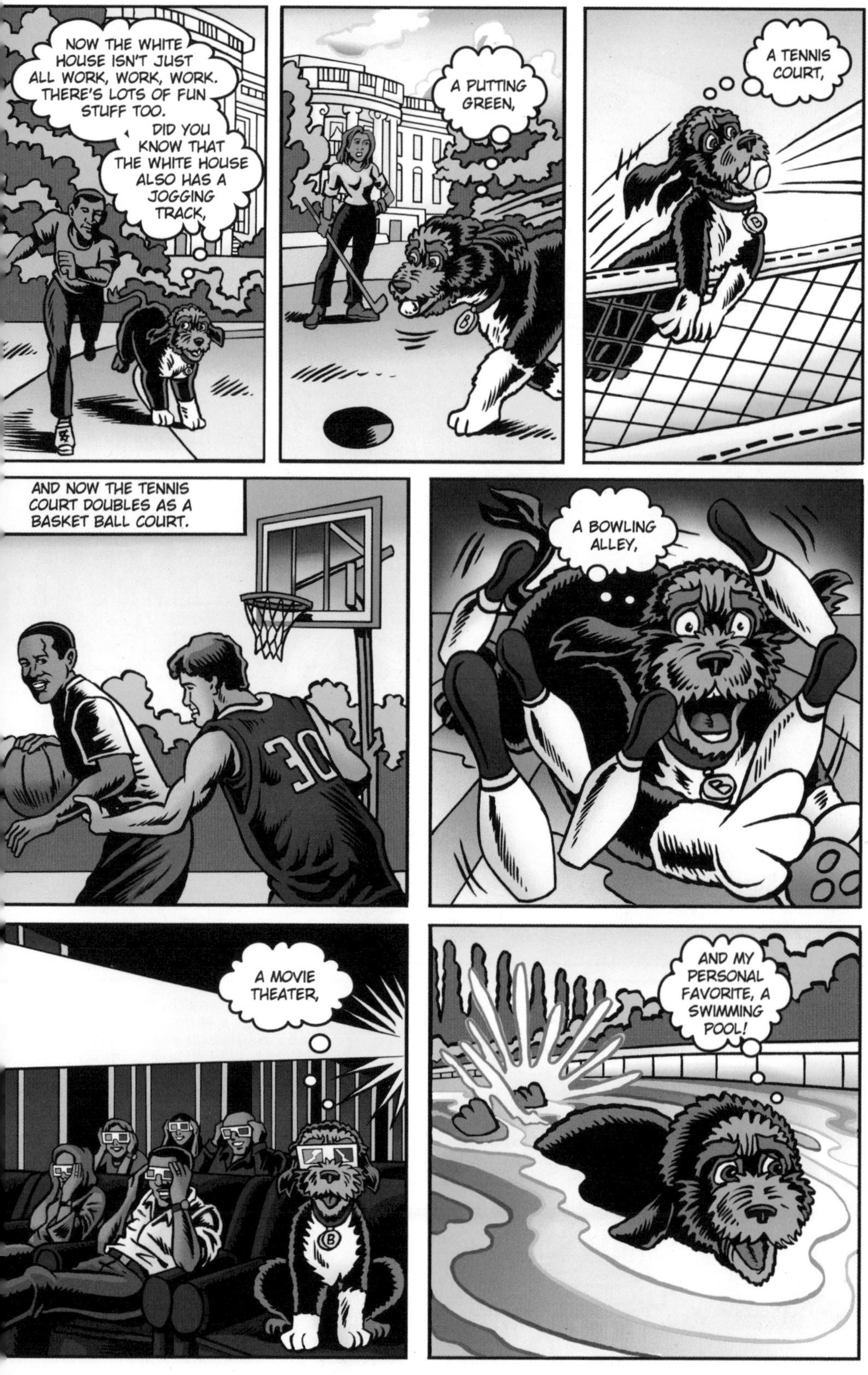
NOW THE WHITE HOUSE ISN'T JUST ALL WORK, WORK, WORK. THERE'S LOTS OF FUN STUFF TOO.
DID YOU KNOW THAT THE WHITE HOUSE ALSO HAS A JOGGING TRACK,
A PUTTING GREEN,
A TENNIS COURT,
AND NOW THE TENNIS COURT DOUBLES AS A BASKET BALL COURT.
30
A BOWLING ALLEY,
A MOVIE THEATER,
AND MY PERSONAL FAVORITE, A SWIMMING POOL!

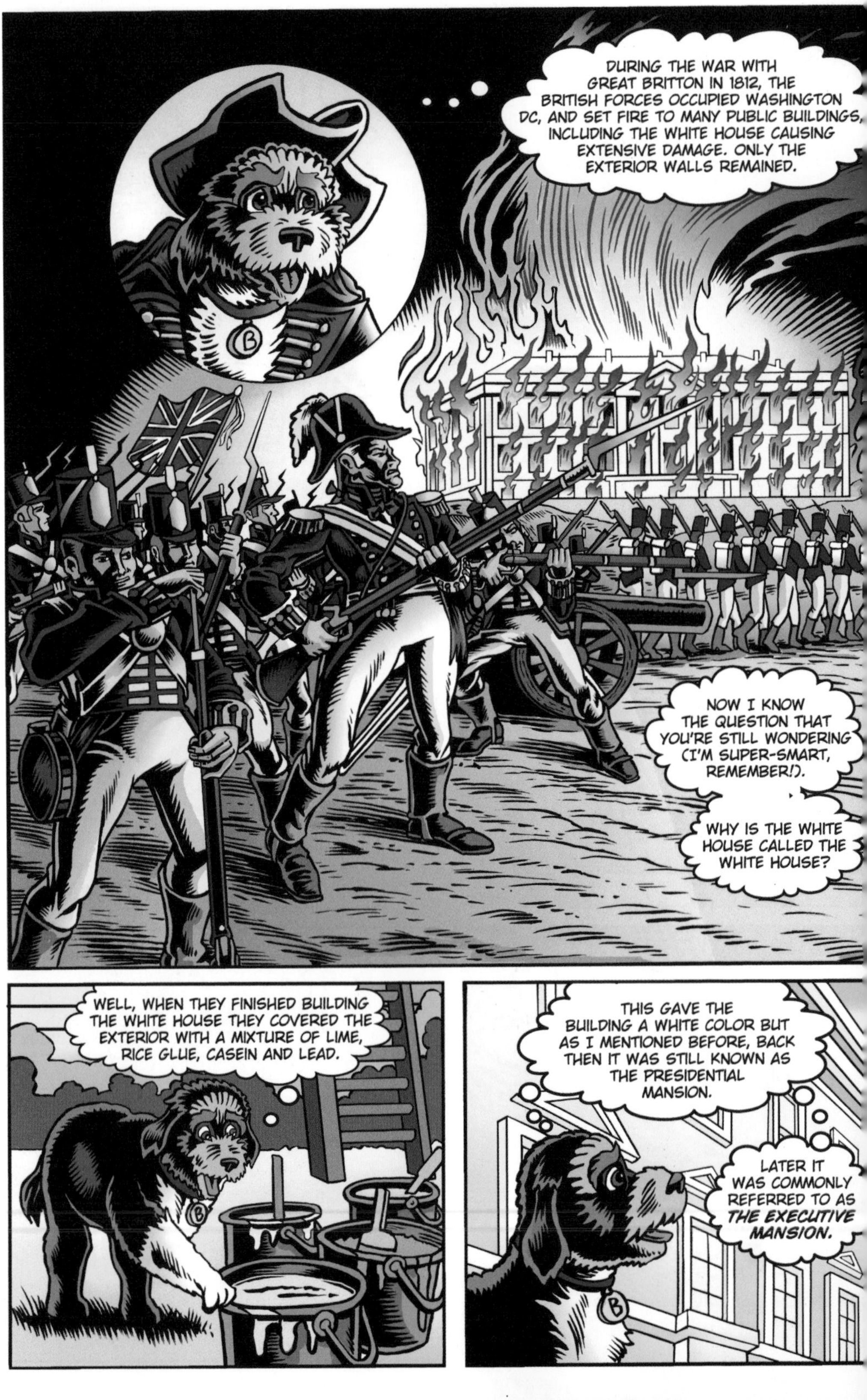
DURING THE WAR WITH GREAT BRITTON IN 1812, THE BRITISH FORCES OCCUPIED WASHINGTON DC, AND SET FIRE TO MANY PUBLIC BUILDINGS, INCLUDING THE WHITE HOUSE CAUSING EXTENSIVE DAMAGE. ONLY THE EXTERIOR WALLS REMAINED.
NOW I KNOW THE QUESTION THAT YOU'RE STILL WONDERING (I'M SUPER-SMART, REMEMBER!).
WHY IS THE WHITE HOUSE CALLED THE WHITE HOUSE?
WELL, WHEN THEY FINISHED BUILDING THE WHITE HOUSE THEY COVERED THE EXTERIOR WITH A MIXTURE OF LIME, RICE GLUE, CASEIN AND LEAD.
THIS GAVE THE BUILDING A WHITE COLOR BUT AS I MENTIONED BEFORE, BACK THEN IT WAS STILL KNOWN AS THE PRESIDENTIAL MANSION.
LATER IT WAS COMMONLY REFERRED TO AS *THE EXECUTIVE MANSION.*

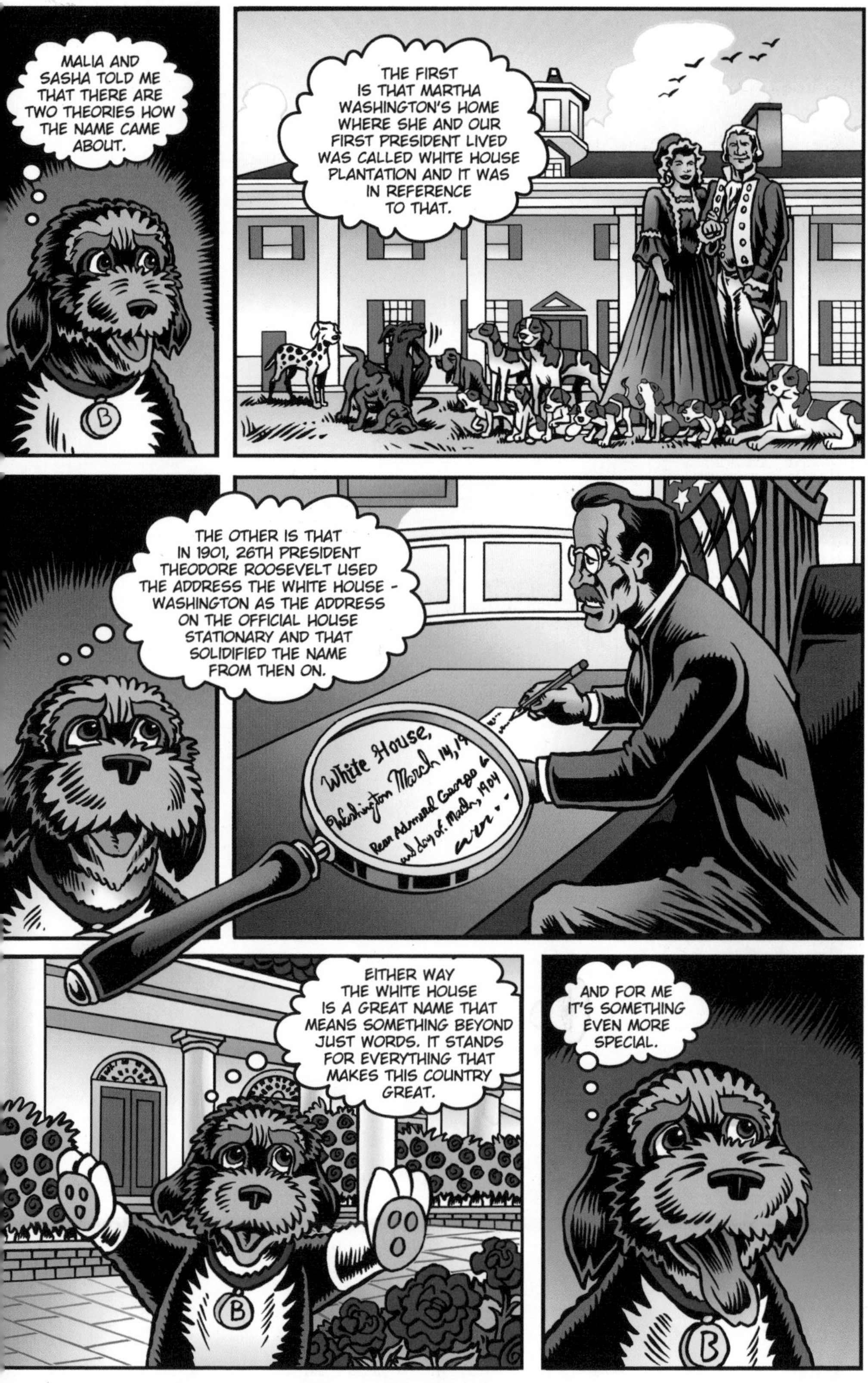
MALIA AND SASHA TOLD ME THAT THERE ARE TWO THEORIES HOW THE NAME CAME ABOUT.
THE FIRST IS THAT MARTHA WASHINGTON'S HOME WHERE SHE AND OUR FIRST PRESIDENT LIVED WAS CALLED WHITE HOUSE PLANTATION AND IT WAS IN REFERENCE TO THAT.
THE OTHER IS THAT IN 1901, 26TH PRESIDENT THEODORE ROOSEVELT USED THE ADDRESS THE WHITE HOUSE - WASHINGTON AS THE ADDRESS ON THE OFFICIAL HOUSE STATIONARY AND THAT SOLIDIFIED THE NAME FROM THEN ON.
White House,
EITHER WAY THE WHITE HOUSE IS A GREAT NAME THAT MEANS SOMETHING BEYOND JUST WORDS. IT STANDS FOR EVERYTHING THAT MAKES THIS COUNTRY GREAT.
AND FOR ME IT'S SOMETHING EVEN MORE SPECIAL.

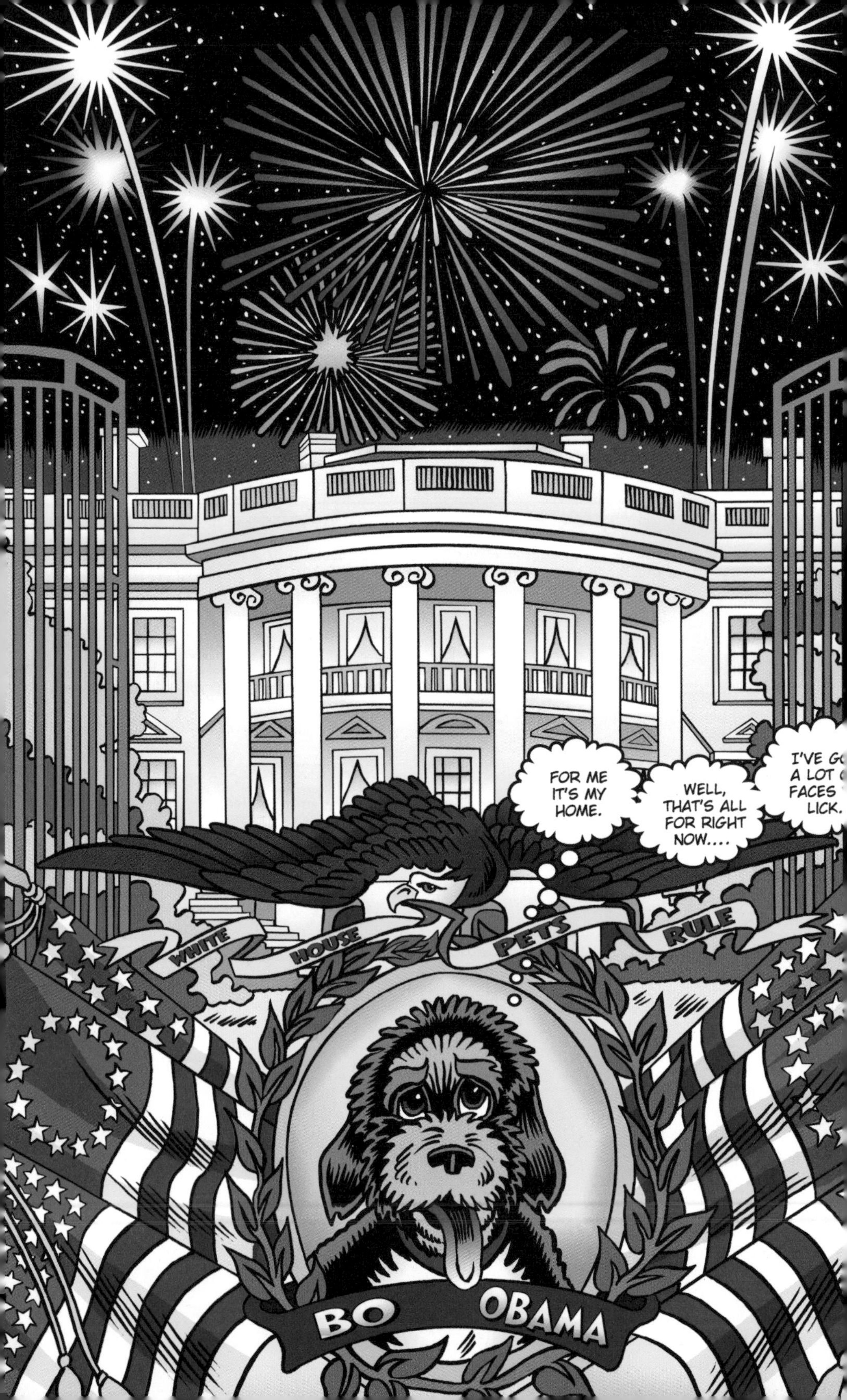

FOR ME IT'S MY HOME.
WELL, THAT'S ALL FOR RIGHT NOW....
I'VE GO A LOT FACES LICK.
WHITE HOUSE PETS RULE
BO OBAMA

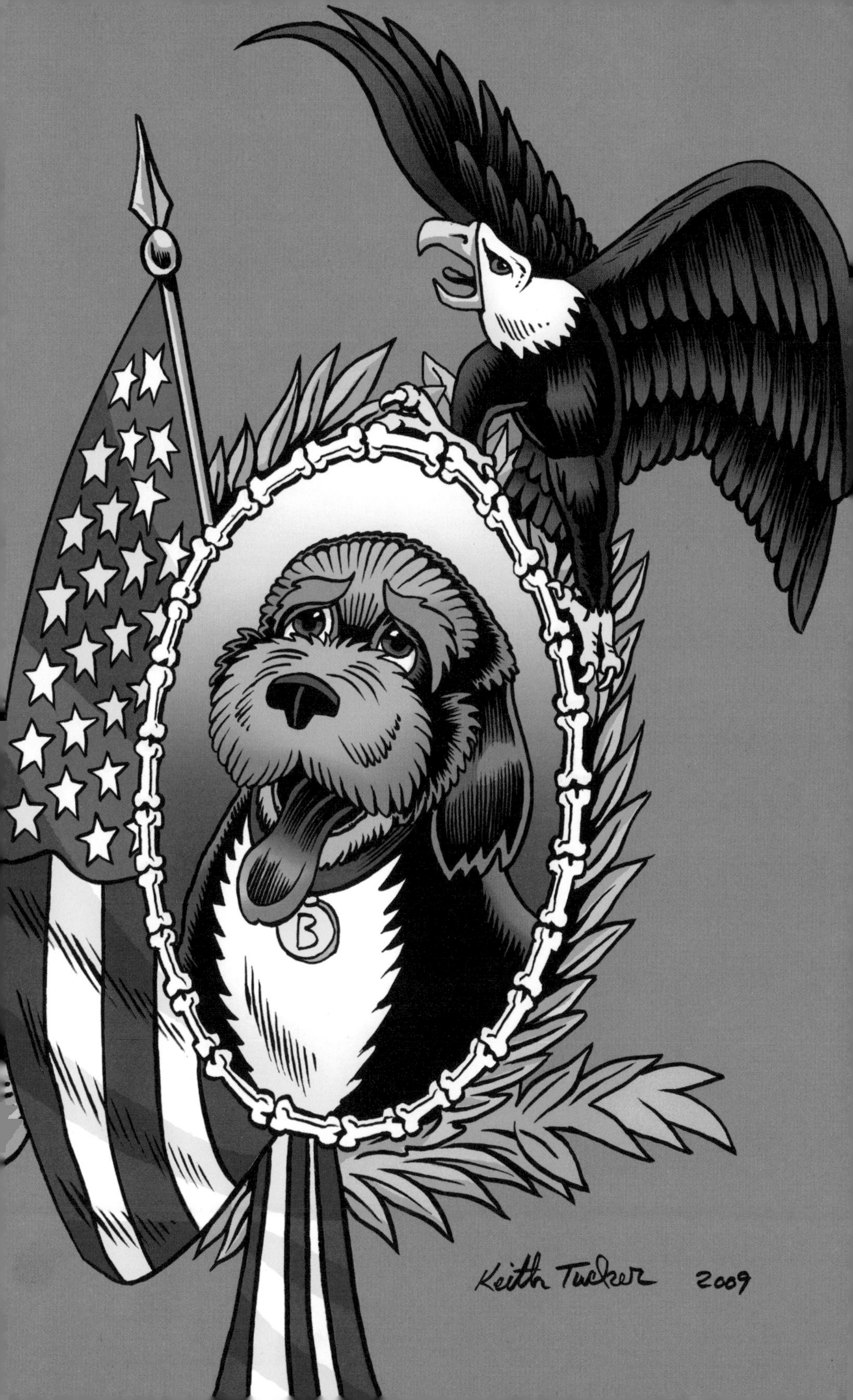
Keith Tucker 2009

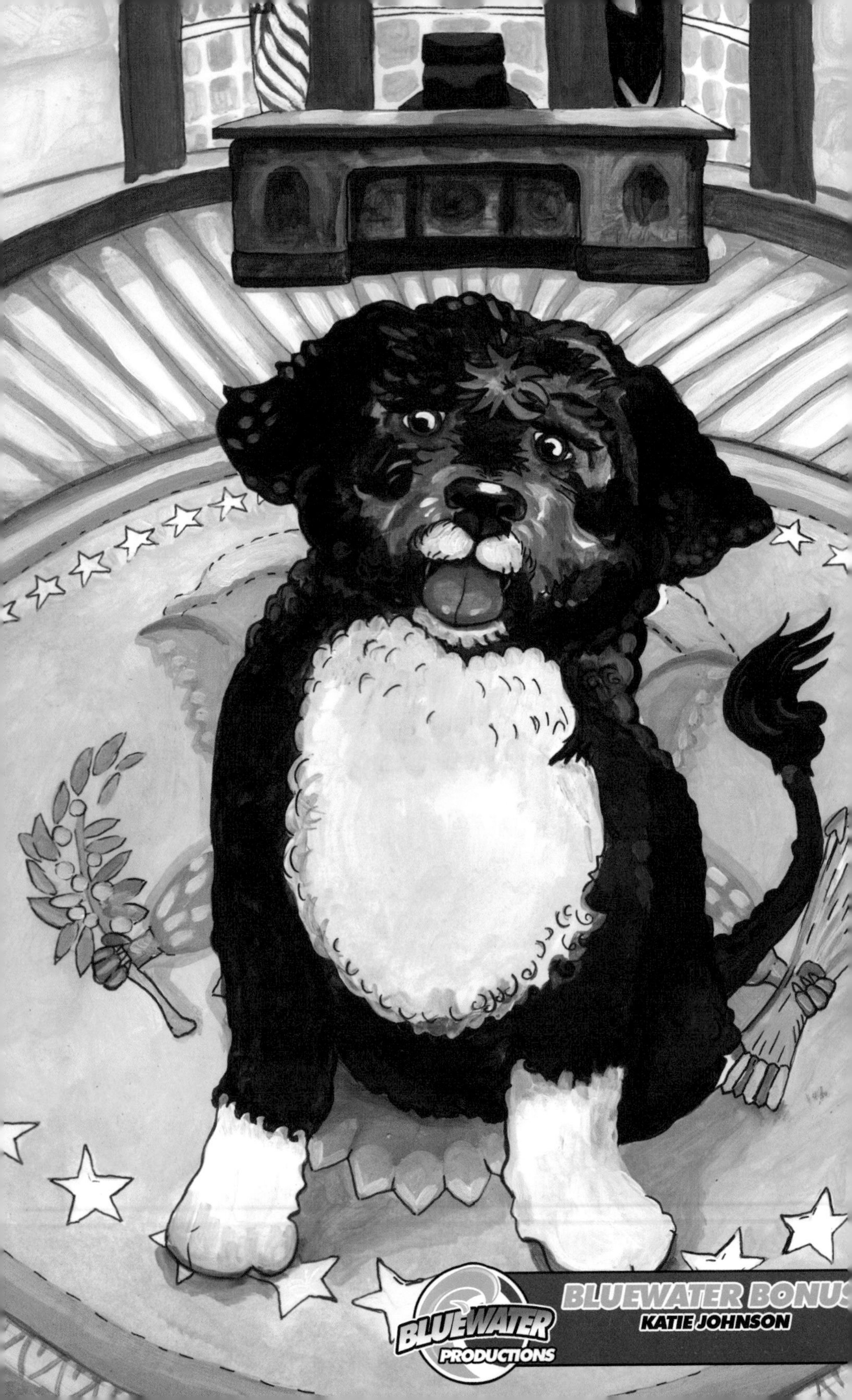
BLUEWATER PRODUCTIONS
BLUEWATER BONUS
KATIE JOHNSON

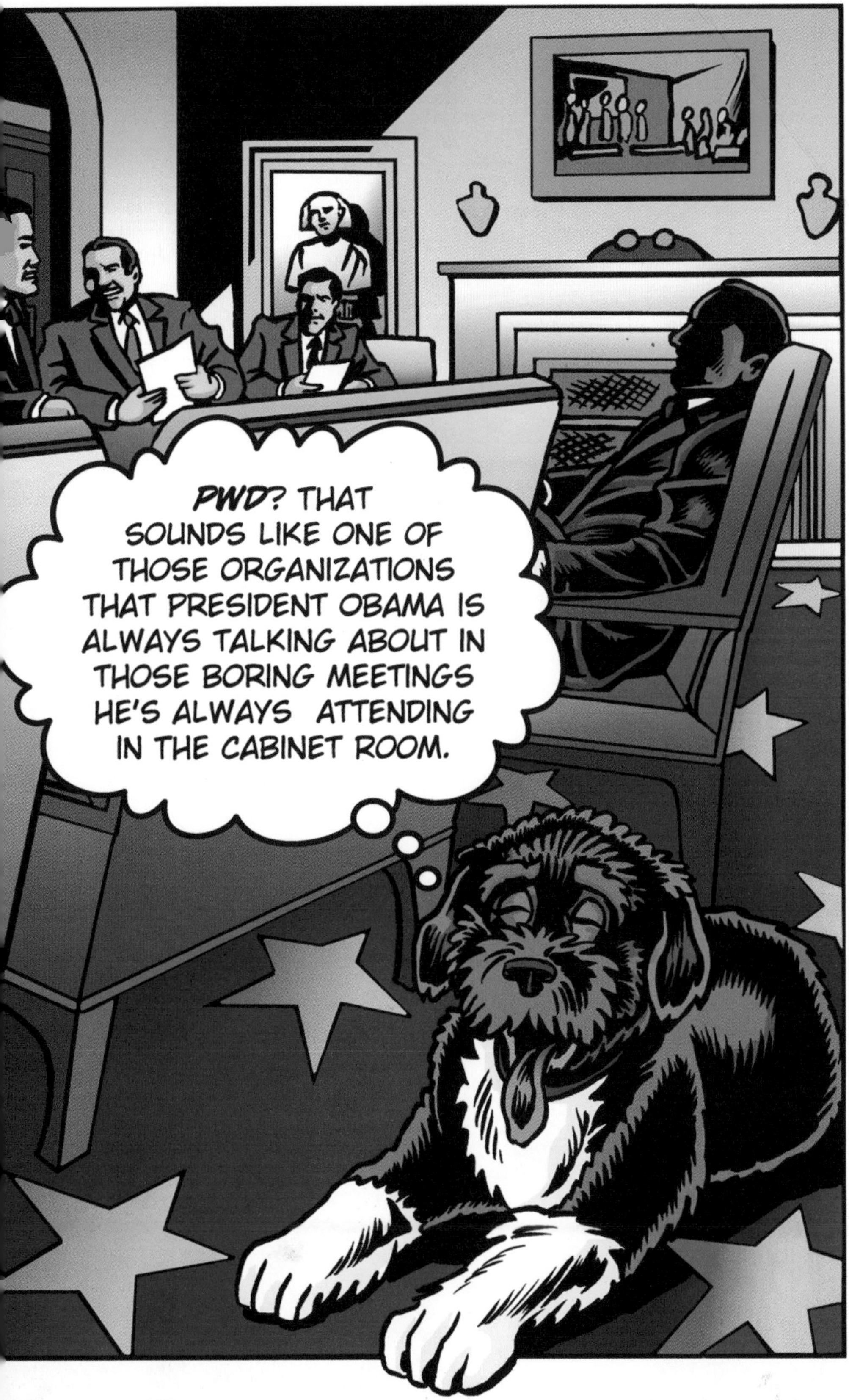
PWD? THAT SOUNDS LIKE ONE OF THOSE ORGANIZATIONS THAT PRESIDENT OBAMA IS ALWAYS TALKING ABOUT IN THOSE BORING MEETINGS HE'S ALWAYS ATTENDING IN THE CABINET ROOM.

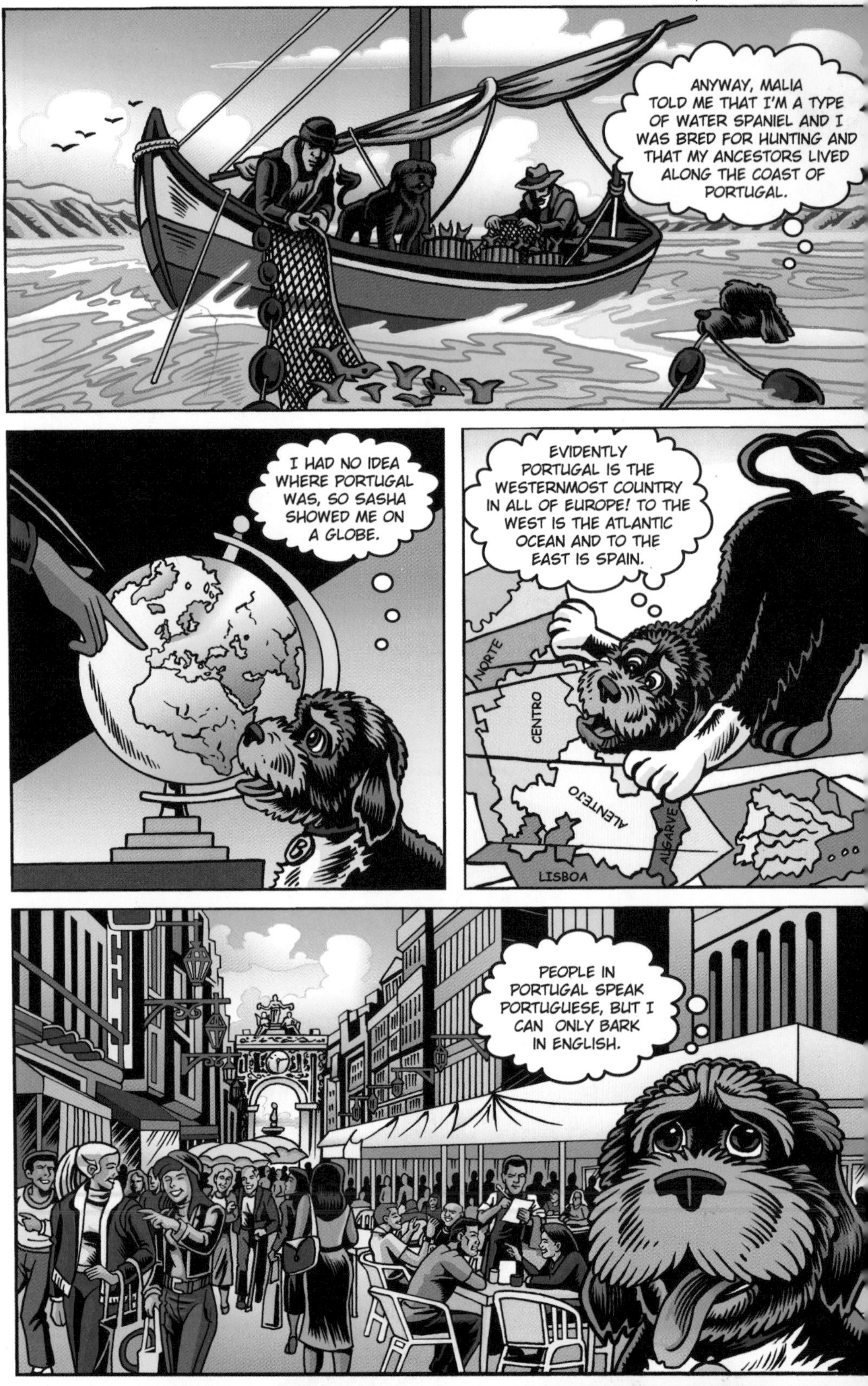
ANYWAY, MALIA TOLD ME THAT I'M A TYPE OF WATER SPANIEL AND I WAS BRED FOR HUNTING AND THAT MY ANCESTORS LIVED ALONG THE COAST OF PORTUGAL.
I HAD NO IDEA WHERE PORTUGAL WAS, SO SASHA SHOWED ME ON A GLOBE.
EVIDENTLY PORTUGAL IS THE WESTERNMOST COUNTRY IN ALL OF EUROPE! TO THE WEST IS THE ATLANTIC OCEAN AND TO THE EAST IS SPAIN.
NORTE
CENTRO
ALENTEJO
ALGARVE
LISBOA
PEOPLE IN PORTUGAL SPEAK PORTUGUESE, BUT I CAN ONLY BARK IN ENGLISH.

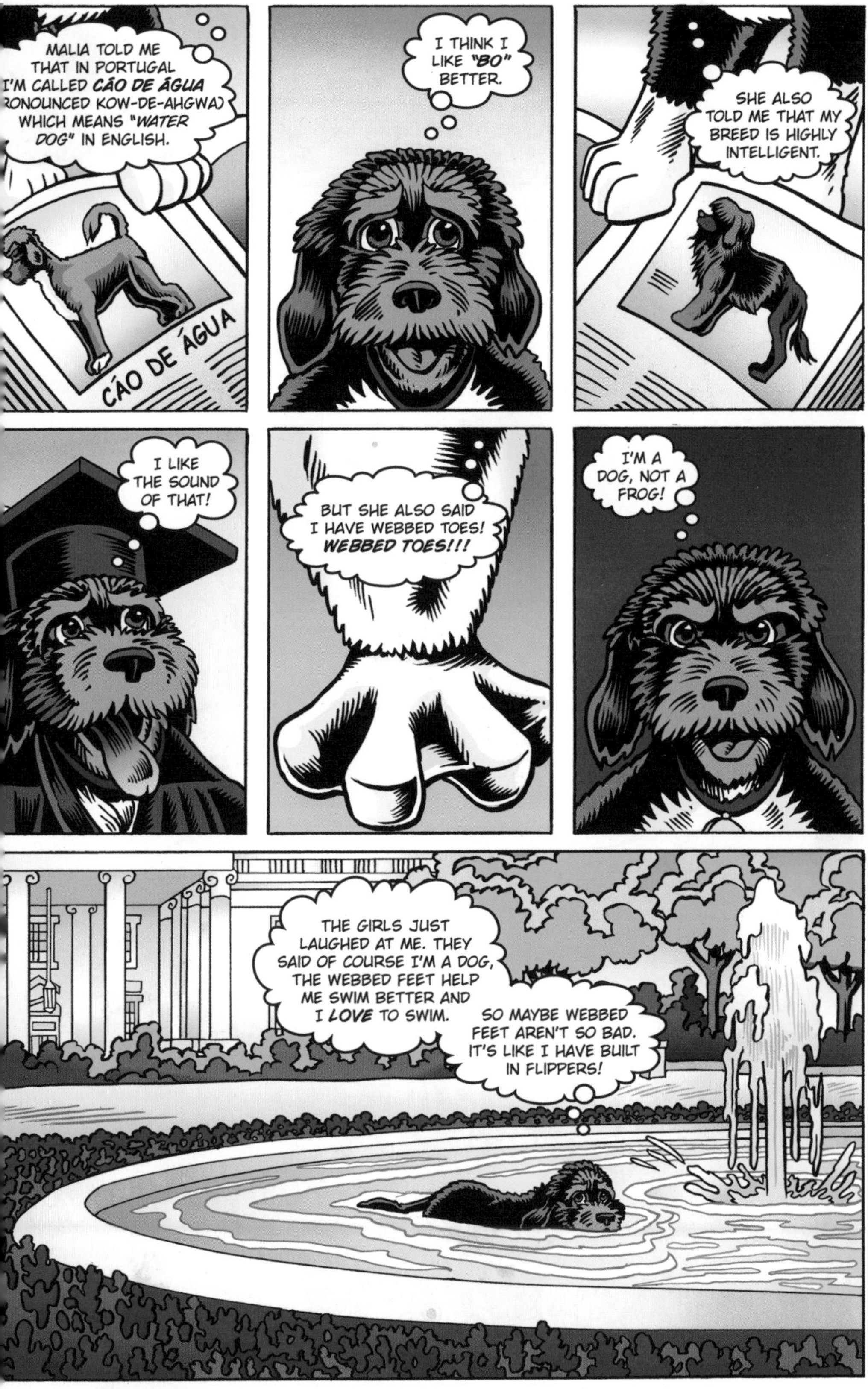
MALIA TOLD ME THAT IN PORTUGAL I'M CALLED ***CÃO DE ÁGUA*** RONOUNCED KOW-DE-AHGWA) WHICH MEANS "*WATER DOG*" IN ENGLISH.
CÁO DE ÁGUA
I THINK I LIKE ***"BO"*** BETTER.
SHE ALSO TOLD ME THAT MY BREED IS HIGHLY INTELLIGENT.
I LIKE THE SOUND OF THAT!
BUT SHE ALSO SAID I HAVE WEBBED TOES! ***WEBBED TOES!!!***
I'M A DOG, NOT A FROG!
THE GIRLS JUST LAUGHED AT ME. THEY SAID OF COURSE I'M A DOG, THE WEBBED FEET HELP ME SWIM BETTER AND I ***LOVE*** TO SWIM.
SO MAYBE WEBBED FEET AREN'T SO BAD. IT'S LIKE I HAVE BUILT IN FLIPPERS!

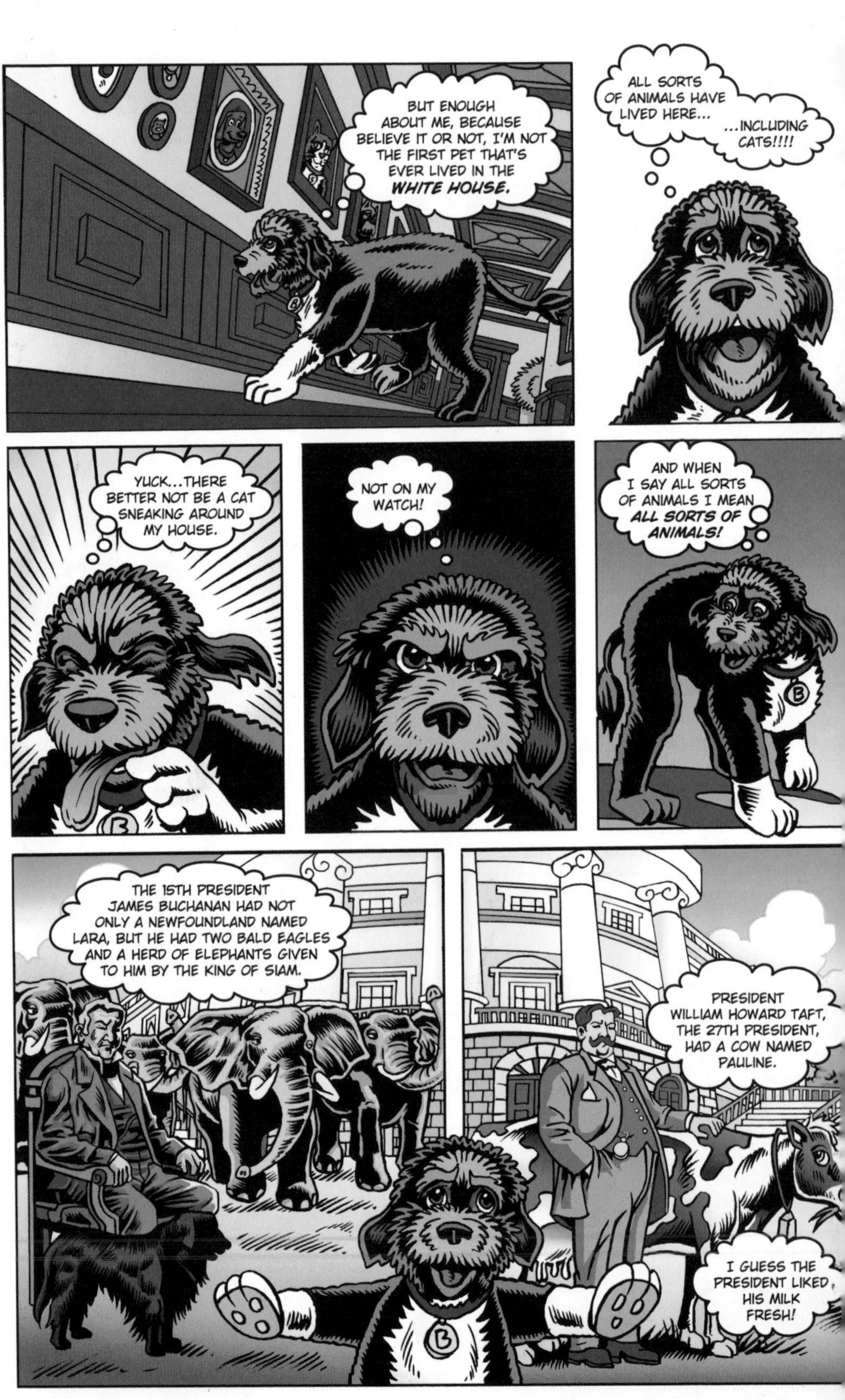
BUT ENOUGH ABOUT ME, BECAUSE BELIEVE IT OR NOT, I'M NOT THE FIRST PET THAT'S EVER LIVED IN THE *WHITE HOUSE.*
ALL SORTS OF ANIMALS HAVE LIVED HERE...
...INCLUDING CATS!!!!
YUCK...THERE BETTER NOT BE A CAT SNEAKING AROUND MY HOUSE.
NOT ON MY WATCH!
AND WHEN I SAY ALL SORTS OF ANIMALS I MEAN *ALL SORTS OF ANIMALS!*
THE 15TH PRESIDENT JAMES BUCHANAN HAD NOT ONLY A NEWFOUNDLAND NAMED LARA, BUT HE HAD TWO BALD EAGLES AND A HERD OF ELEPHANTS GIVEN TO HIM BY THE KING OF SIAM.
PRESIDENT WILLIAM HOWARD TAFT, THE 27TH PRESIDENT, HAD A COW NAMED PAULINE.
I GUESS THE PRESIDENT LIKED HIS MILK FRESH!

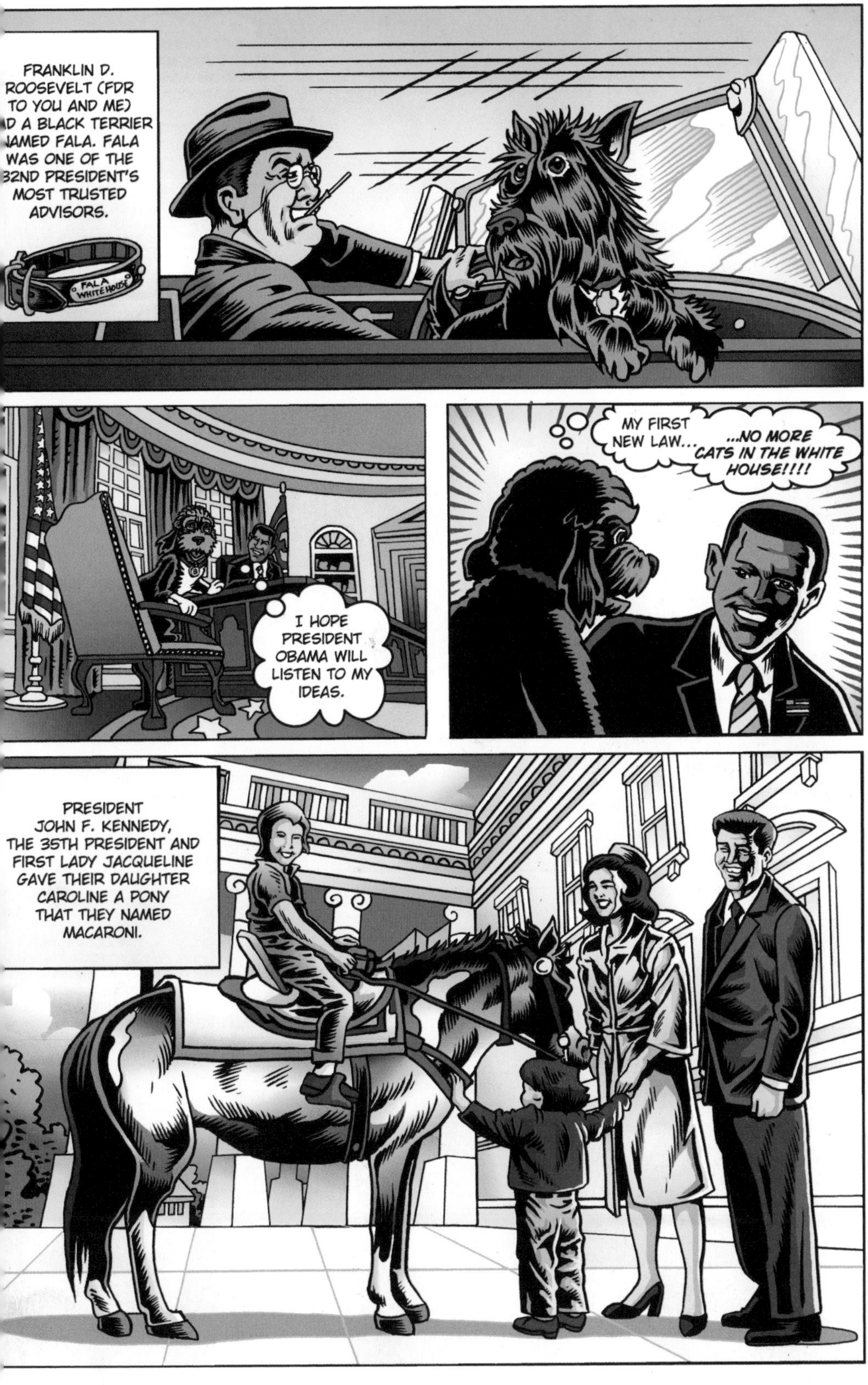
FRANKLIN D. ROOSEVELT (FDR TO YOU AND ME) D A BLACK TERRIER JAMED FALA. FALA WAS ONE OF THE 32ND PRESIDENT'S MOST TRUSTED ADVISORS.
FALA WHITE HOUSE
I HOPE PRESIDENT OBAMA WILL LISTEN TO MY IDEAS.
MY FIRST NEW LAW...
...NO MORE CATS IN THE WHITE HOUSE!!!!
PRESIDENT JOHN F. KENNEDY, THE 35TH PRESIDENT AND FIRST LADY JACQUELINE GAVE THEIR DAUGHTER CAROLINE A PONY THAT THEY NAMED MACARONI.

MACARONI?! WHO NAMES THEIR PET AFTER FOOD?

THEY TOLD ME THAT I WAS NAMED AFTER THE MUSICIAN BO DIDDLY.

NOW THAT'S A NAMESAKE!

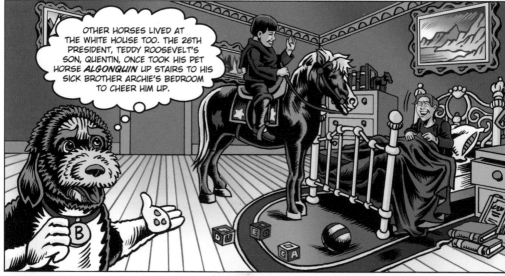

OTHER HORSES LIVED AT THE WHITE HOUSE TOO. THE 26TH PRESIDENT, TEDDY ROOSEVELT'S SON, QUENTIN, ONCE TOOK HIS PET HORSE *ALGONQUIN* UP STAIRS TO HIS SICK BROTHER ARCHIE'S BEDROOM TO CHEER HIM UP.

THERE WAS EVEN AN OUTER SPACE PUPPY, *"PUSHINKA"*. A GIFT TO PRESIDENT KENNEDY'S DAUGHTER CAROLINE FROM SOVIET LEADER NIKITA KHRUSCHEV.

PUSHINKA'S MOM, *"LAIKA"* WAS A GENUINE CANINE SPACE HERO WH ORBITED THE EARTH IN 1957, ONBOARD SPUTNIK FIVE.

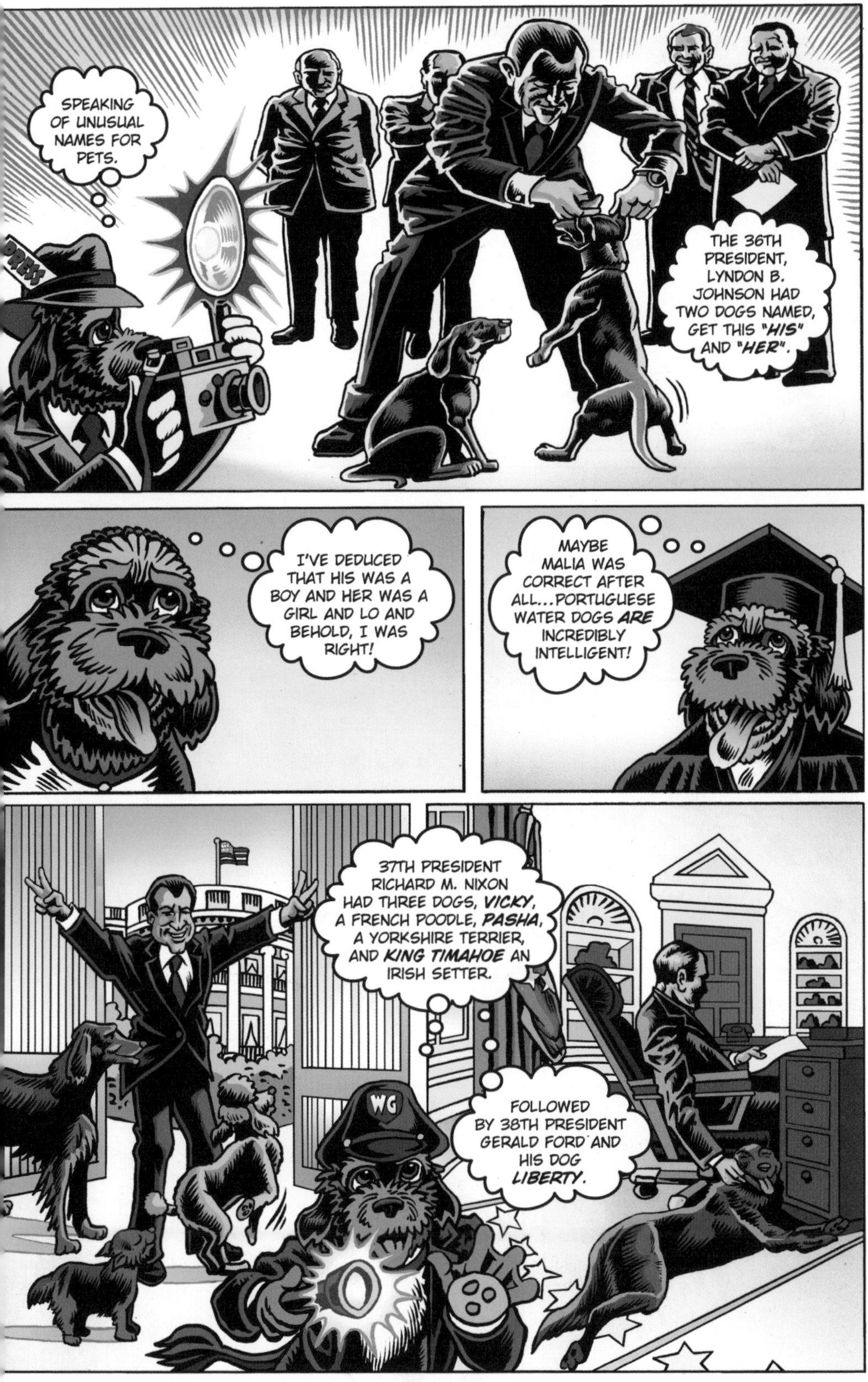
SPEAKING OF UNUSUAL NAMES FOR PETS.
PRESS
THE 36TH PRESIDENT, LYNDON B. JOHNSON HAD TWO DOGS NAMED, GET THIS "HIS" AND "HER".
I'VE DEDUCED THAT HIS WAS A BOY AND HER WAS A GIRL AND LO AND BEHOLD, I WAS RIGHT!
MAYBE MALIA WAS CORRECT AFTER ALL...PORTUGUESE WATER DOGS ARE INCREDIBLY INTELLIGENT!
37TH PRESIDENT RICHARD M. NIXON HAD THREE DOGS, VICKY, A FRENCH POODLE, PASHA, A YORKSHIRE TERRIER, AND KING TIMAHOE AN IRISH SETTER.
WG
FOLLOWED BY 38TH PRESIDENT GERALD FORD AND HIS DOG LIBERTY.

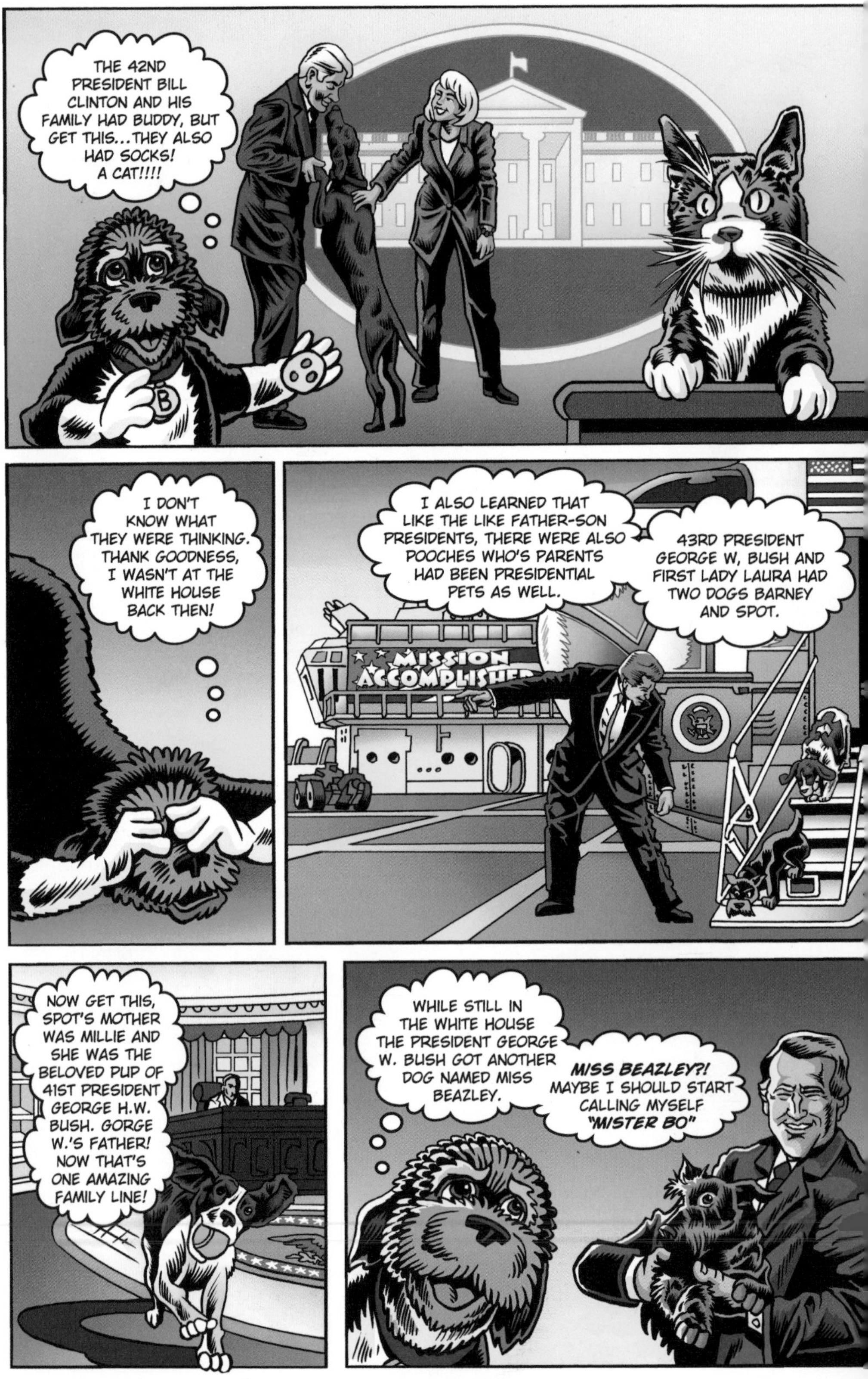
THE 42ND PRESIDENT BILL CLINTON AND HIS FAMILY HAD BUDDY, BUT GET THIS...THEY ALSO HAD SOCKS! A CAT!!!!
I DON'T KNOW WHAT THEY WERE THINKING. THANK GOODNESS, I WASN'T AT THE WHITE HOUSE BACK THEN!
I ALSO LEARNED THAT LIKE THE LIKE FATHER-SON PRESIDENTS, THERE WERE ALSO POOCHES WHO'S PARENTS HAD BEEN PRESIDENTIAL PETS AS WELL.
43RD PRESIDENT GEORGE W, BUSH AND FIRST LADY LAURA HAD TWO DOGS BARNEY AND SPOT.
MISSION ACCOMPLISHED
NOW GET THIS, SPOT'S MOTHER WAS MILLIE AND SHE WAS THE BELOVED PUP OF 41ST PRESIDENT GEORGE H.W. BUSH. GORGE W.'S FATHER! NOW THAT'S ONE AMAZING FAMILY LINE!
WHILE STILL IN THE WHITE HOUSE THE PRESIDENT GEORGE W. BUSH GOT ANOTHER DOG NAMED MISS BEAZLEY.
MISS BEAZLEY?! MAYBE I SHOULD START CALLING MYSELF "MISTER BO"

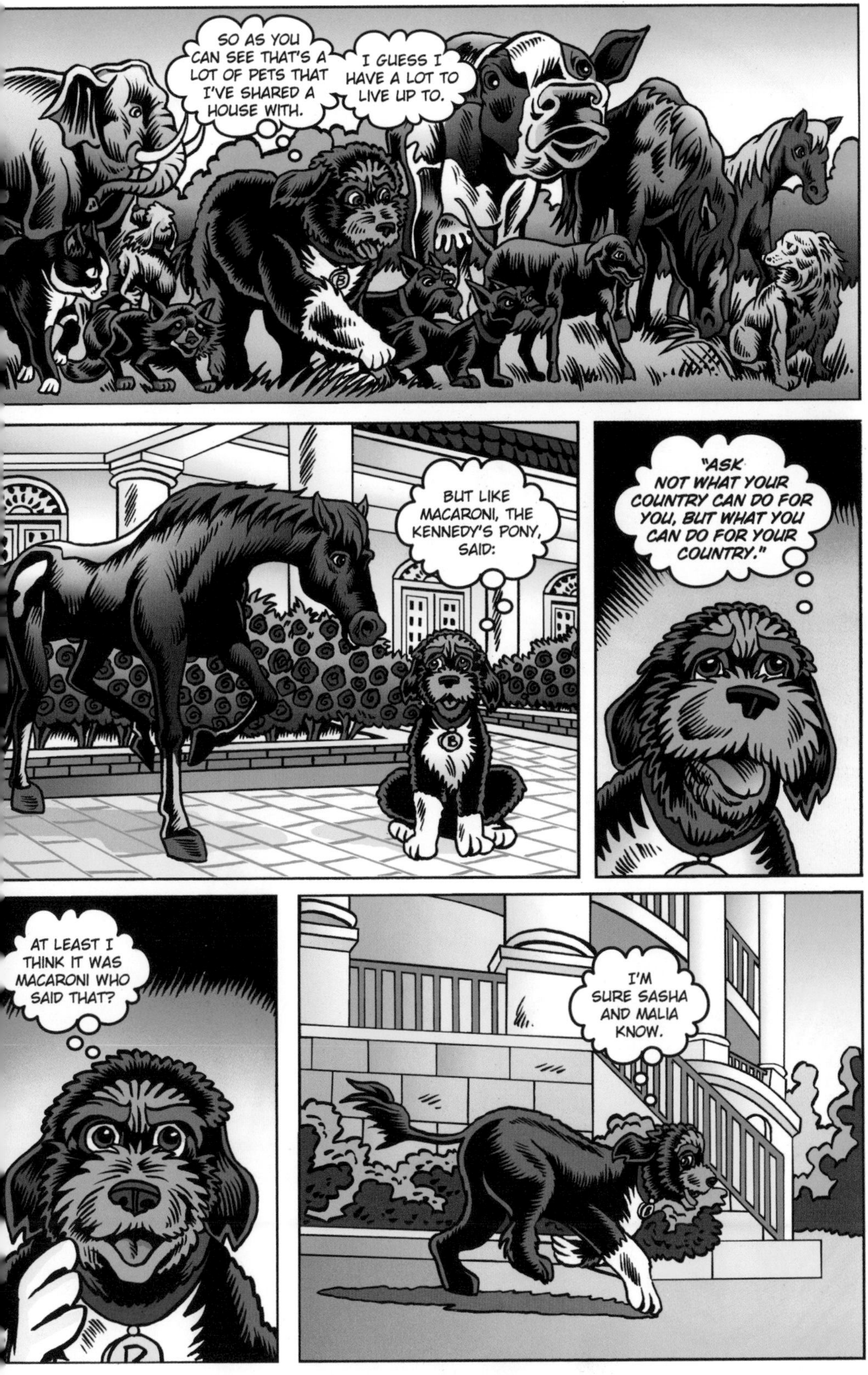
SO AS YOU CAN SEE THAT'S A LOT OF PETS THAT I'VE SHARED A HOUSE WITH.
I GUESS I HAVE A LOT TO LIVE UP TO.
BUT LIKE MACARONI, THE KENNEDY'S PONY, SAID:
"ASK NOT WHAT YOUR COUNTRY CAN DO FOR YOU, BUT WHAT YOU CAN DO FOR YOUR COUNTRY."
AT LEAST I THINK IT WAS MACARONI WHO SAID THAT?
I'M SURE SASHA AND MALIA KNOW.

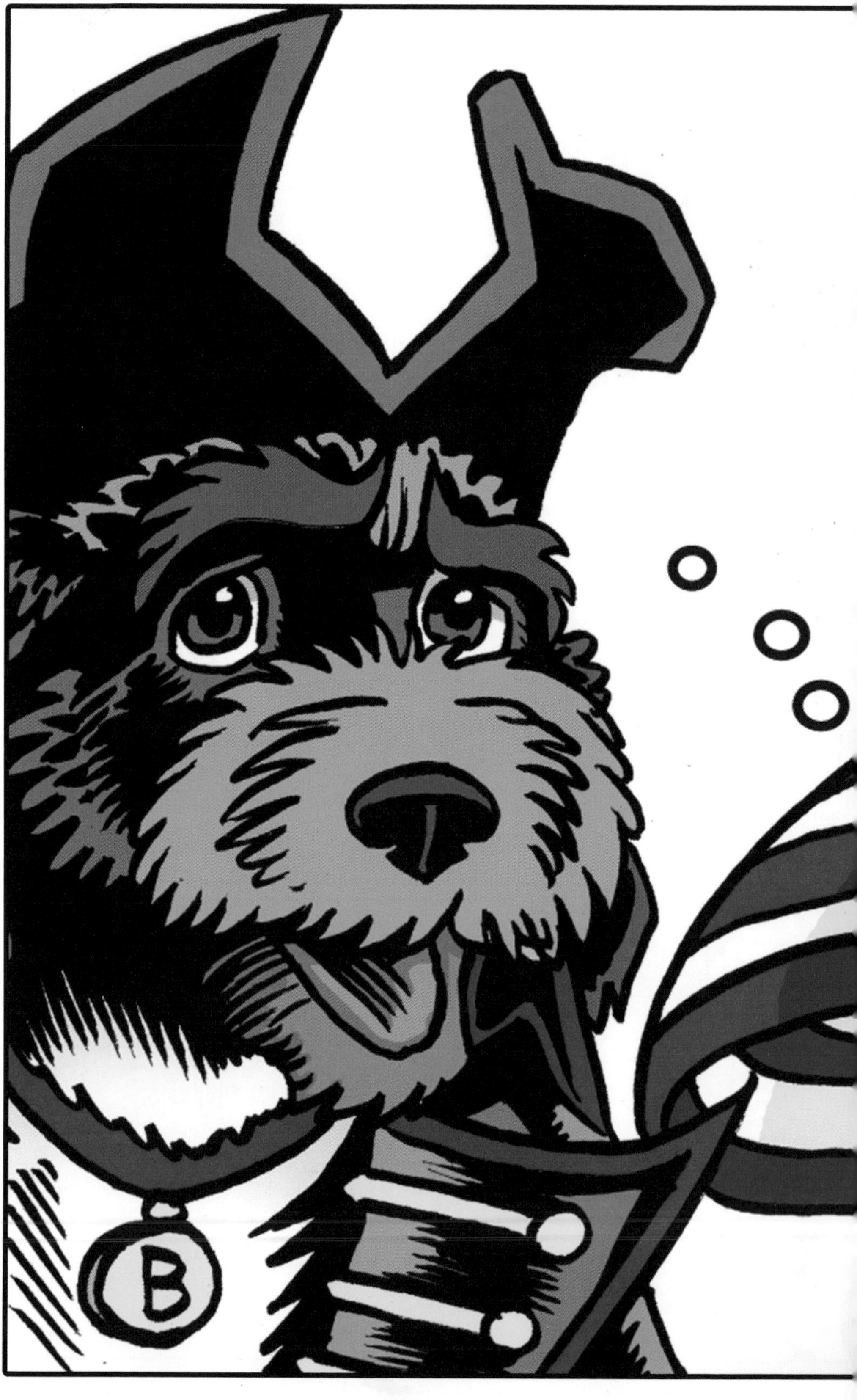
B

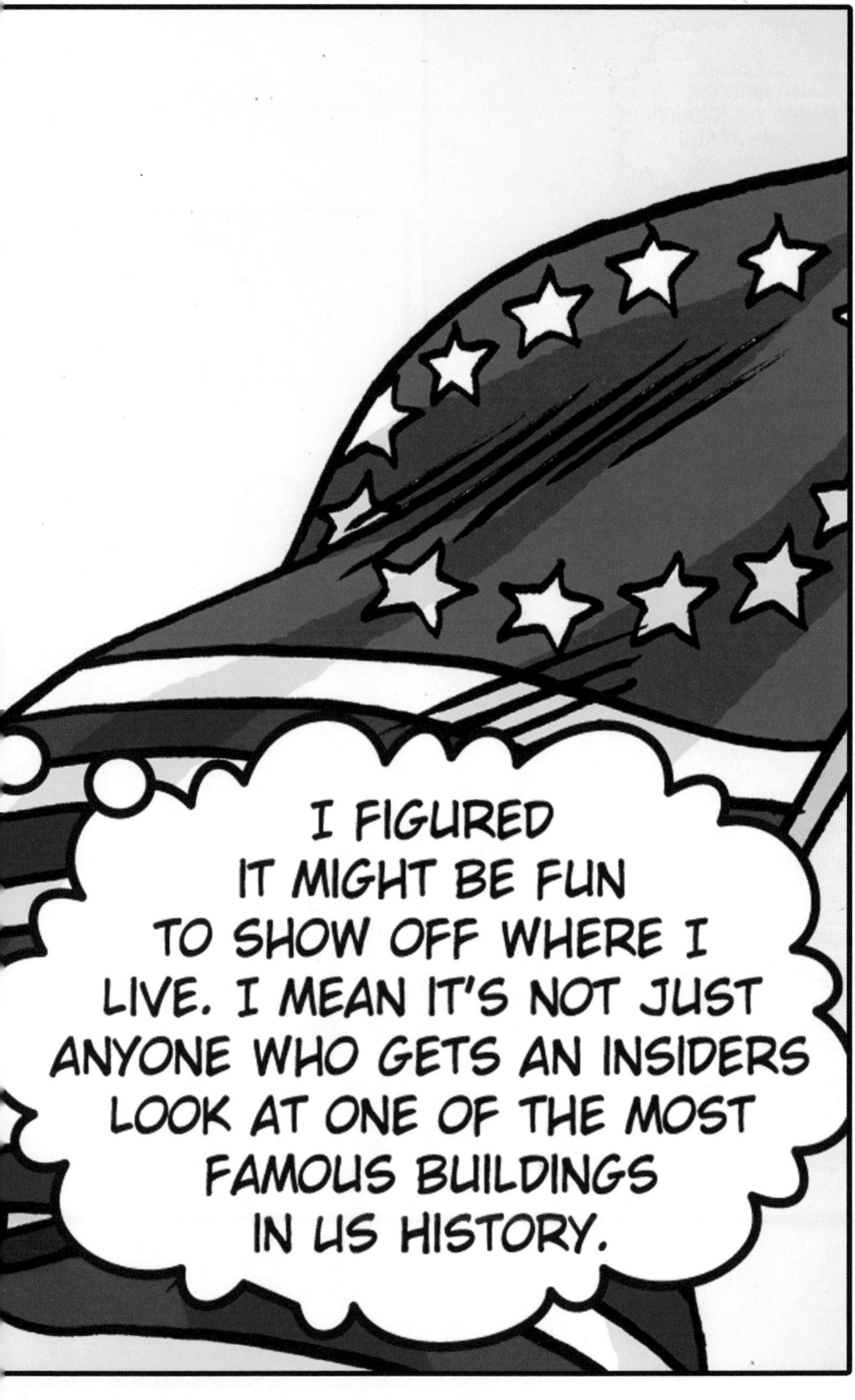
I FIGURED IT MIGHT BE FUN TO SHOW OFF WHERE I LIVE. I MEAN IT'S NOT JUST ANYONE WHO GETS AN INSIDERS LOOK AT ONE OF THE MOST FAMOUS BUILDINGS IN US HISTORY.

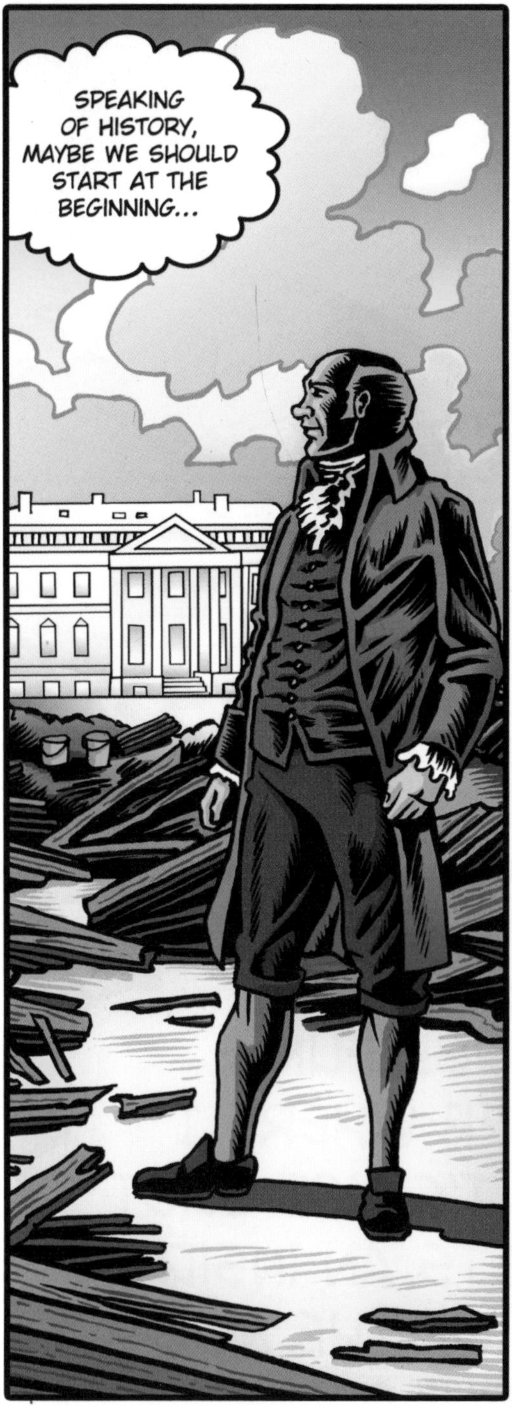
SPEAKING OF HISTORY, MAYBE WE SHOULD START AT THE BEGINNING...

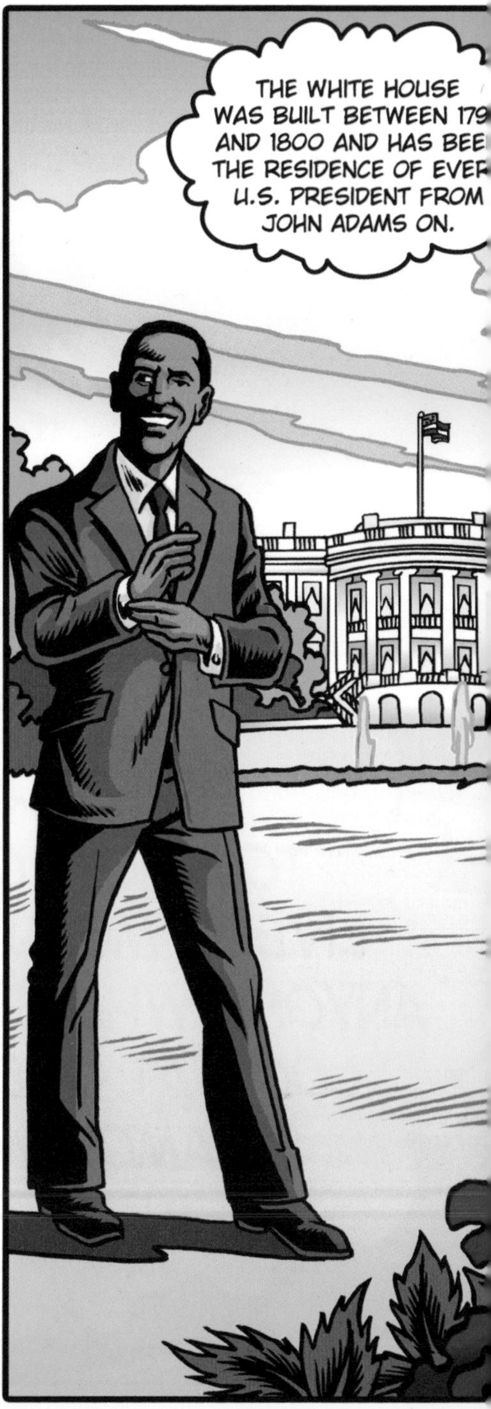
THE WHITE HOUSE
WAS BUILT BETWEEN 179
AND 1800 AND HAS BEE
THE RESIDENCE OF EVER
U.S. PRESIDENT FROM
JOHN ADAMS ON.

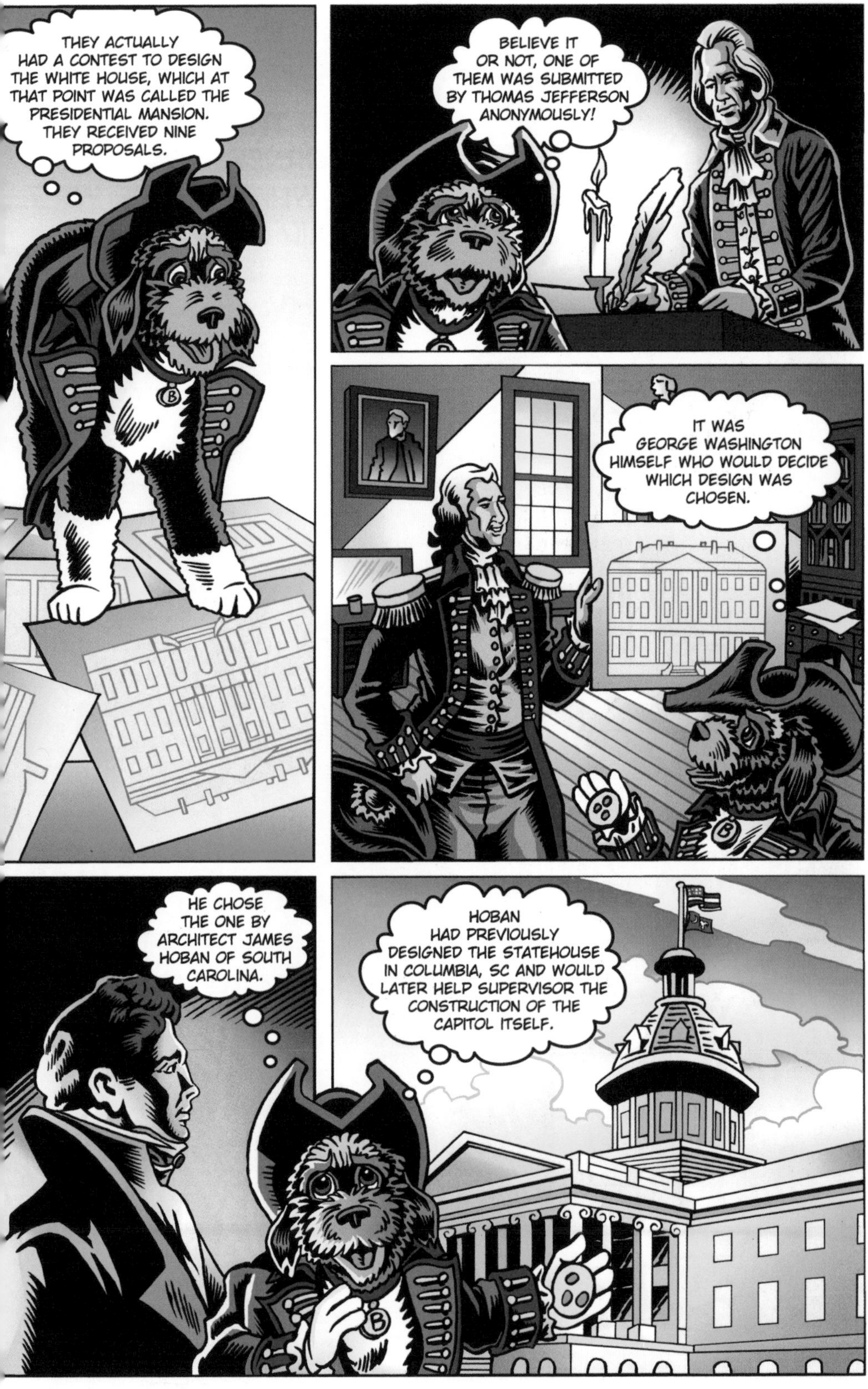
THEY ACTUALLY HAD A CONTEST TO DESIGN THE WHITE HOUSE, WHICH AT THAT POINT WAS CALLED THE PRESIDENTIAL MANSION. THEY RECEIVED NINE PROPOSALS.
BELIEVE IT OR NOT, ONE OF THEM WAS SUBMITTED BY THOMAS JEFFERSON ANONYMOUSLY!
IT WAS GEORGE WASHINGTON HIMSELF WHO WOULD DECIDE WHICH DESIGN WAS CHOSEN.
HE CHOSE THE ONE BY ARCHITECT JAMES HOBAN OF SOUTH CAROLINA.
HOBAN HAD PREVIOUSLY DESIGNED THE STATEHOUSE IN COLUMBIA, SC AND WOULD LATER HELP SUPERVISOR THE CONSTRUCTION OF THE CAPITOL ITSELF.

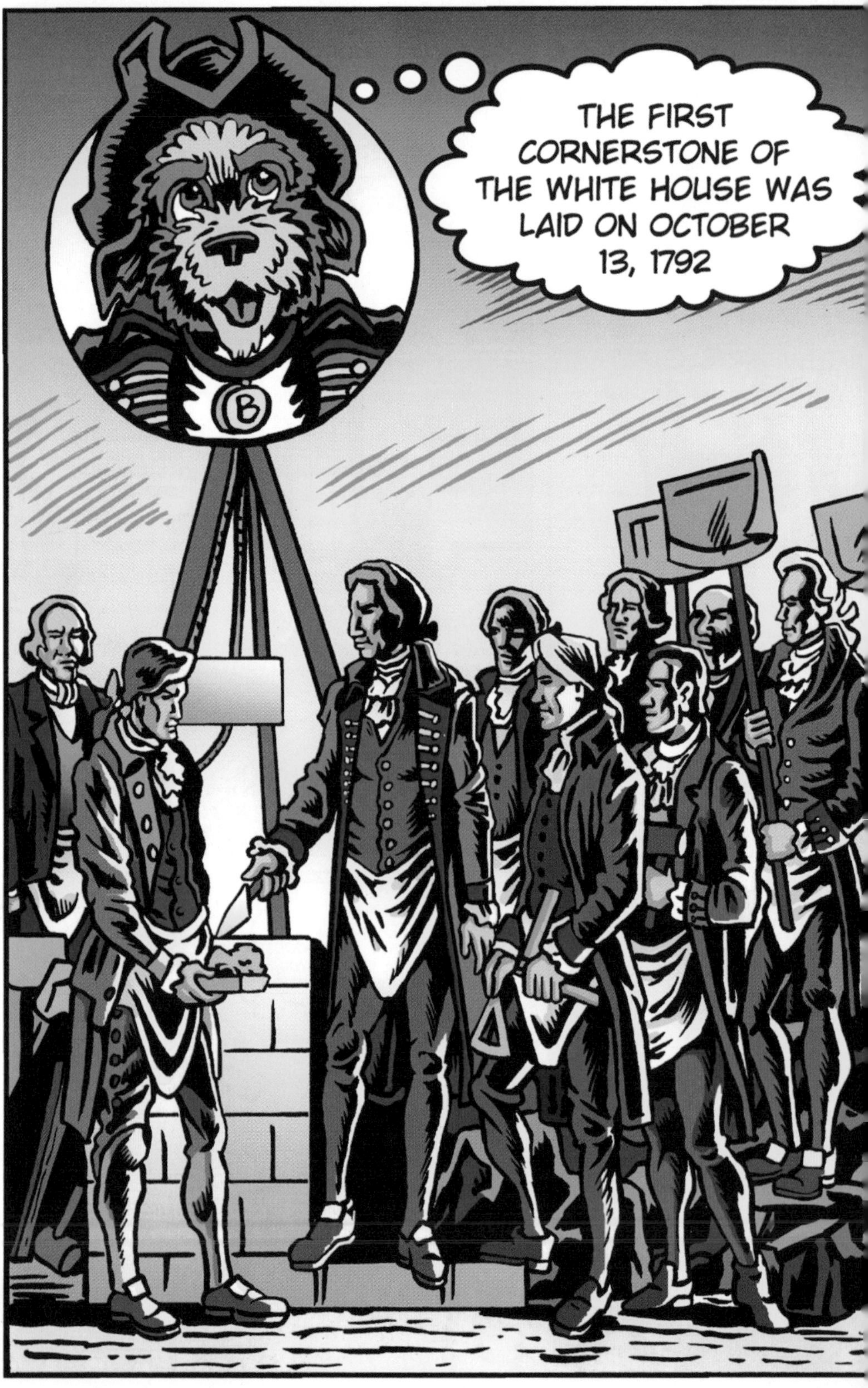
THE FIRST CORNERSTONE OF THE WHITE HOUSE WAS LAID ON OCTOBER 13, 1792

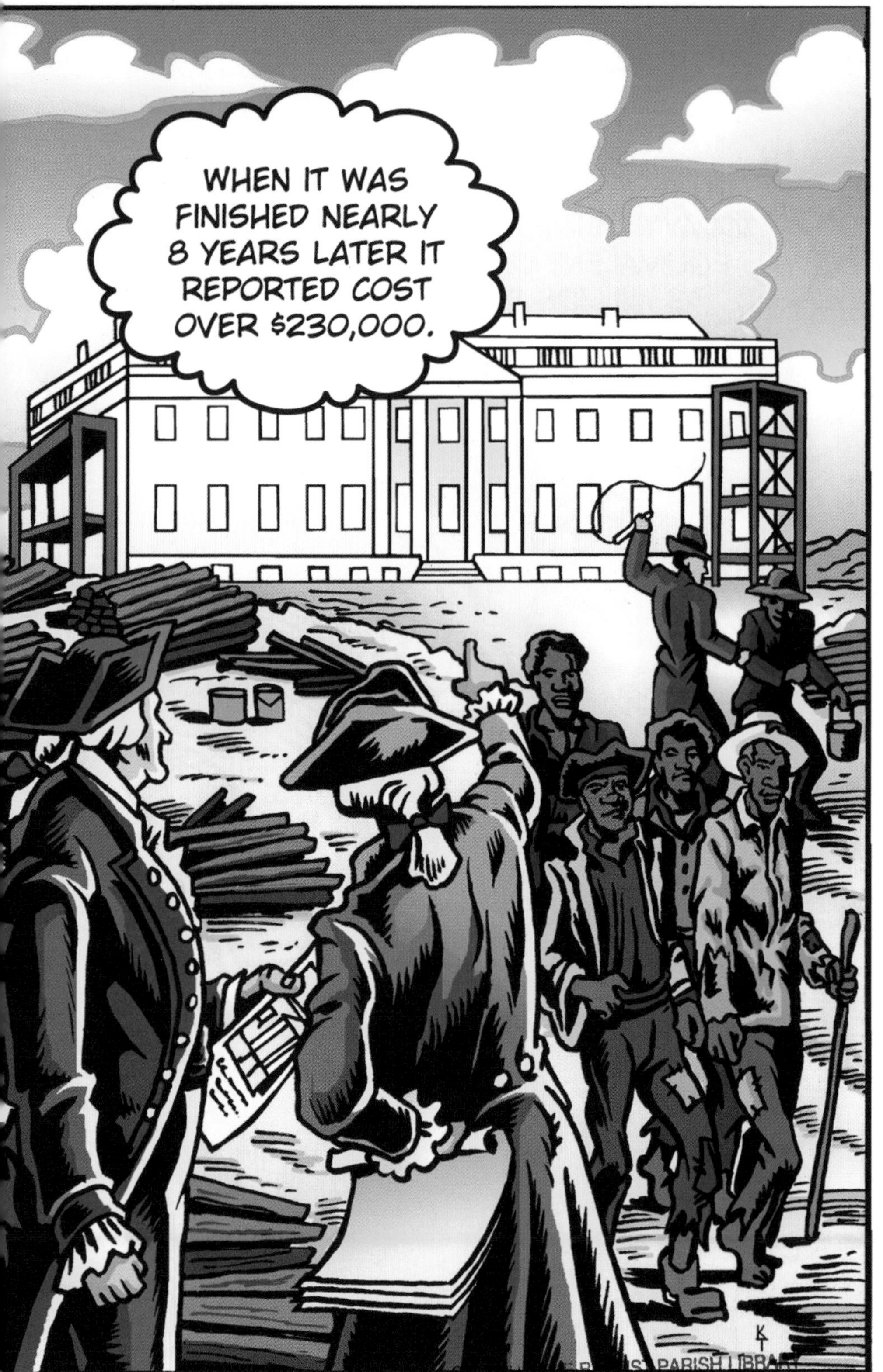
WHEN IT WAS FINISHED NEARLY 8 YEARS LATER IT REPORTED COST OVER $230,000.

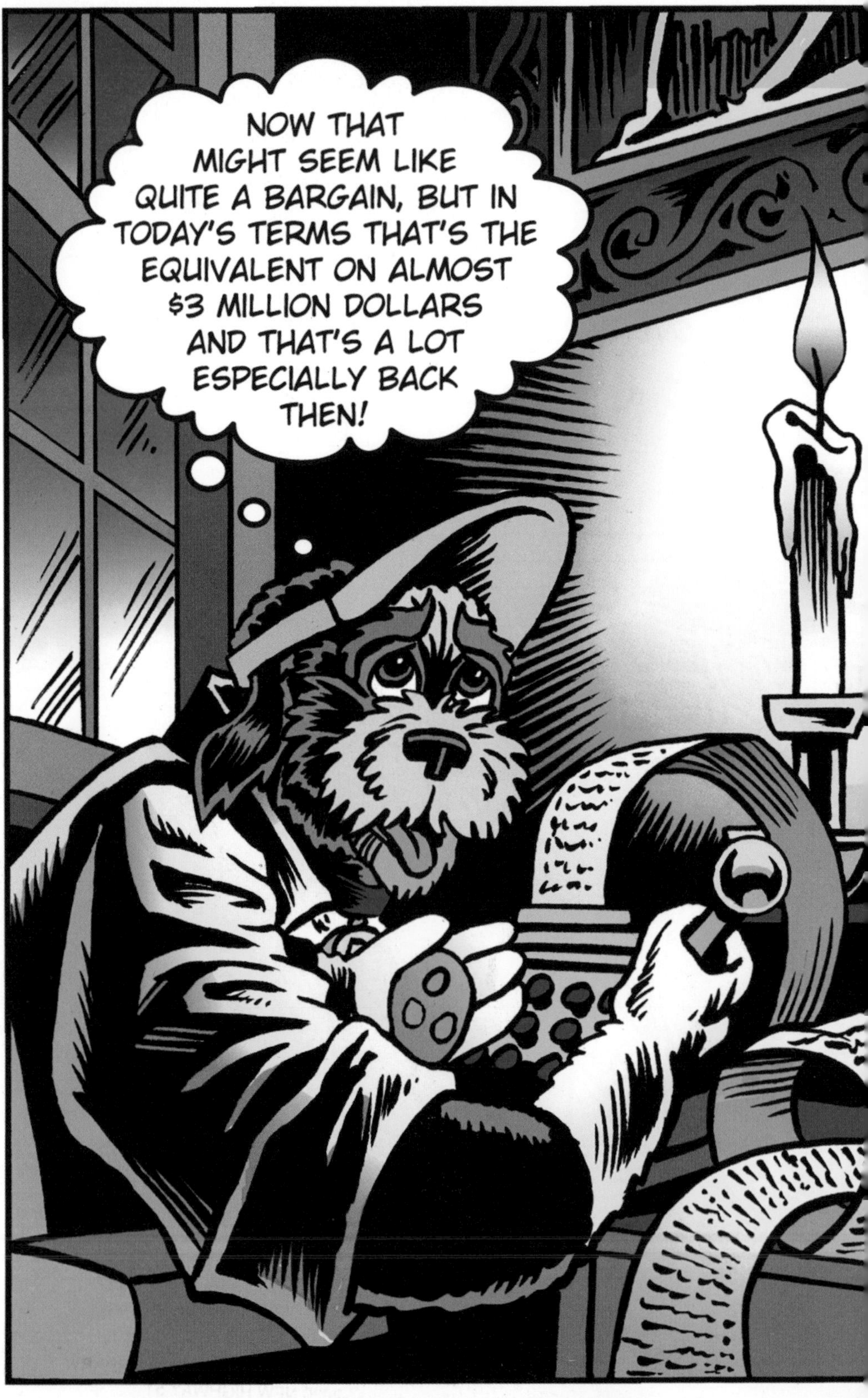
NOW THAT MIGHT SEEM LIKE QUITE A BARGAIN, BUT IN TODAY'S TERMS THAT'S THE EQUIVALENT ON ALMOST $3 MILLION DOLLARS AND THAT'S A LOT ESPECIALLY BACK THEN!